ACTIVITY & TEST PREP WORKBOOK

SIDE by SIDE

THIRD EDITION

Steven J. Molinsky • Bill Bliss

with

Carolyn Graham • Peter S. Bliss

Contributing Authors

Dorothy Lynde • Elizabeth Handley

Illustrated by

Richard E. Hill

BOOK 1

Longman

HARRISON COMMUNITY EDUCATION
ESL Program / SMRC
1118 South Harrison Road
East Lansing, Michigan 48823 USA
Telephone (517) 337-8353

TO THE TEACHER

This enhanced edition of *Side by Side Activity Workbook 1* includes practice tests designed to prepare students for the types of standardized tests and performance assessments used by many instructional programs to measure and report students' progress. A practice test for each chapter of the series simultaneously assesses students' achievement of the chapter's instructional objectives, provides intensified coverage of lifeskill competencies, and prepares students for standardized general language proficiency tests that assess students' educational advancement and reflect programs' effectiveness in meeting outcome-based performance standards.

The practice tests appear in the second section of this workbook on pages T1–T58. They include: multiple-choice questions that assess vocabulary, grammar, reading, and listening skills; short-answer questions that cover lifeskill competencies and basic literacy tasks (such as reading medicine labels and filling out forms); writing assessments that can be evaluated using a standardized scoring rubric and collected in portfolios of students' work; and speaking performance assessments designed to stimulate face-to-face interactions between students, for evaluation by the teacher using a standardized scoring rubric, or for self-evaluation by students.

Pages are perforated so that completed tests can be handed in and can serve as a record of students' participation and progress in the instructional program. Scripts for the listening assessment activities are included at the end of this volume and may be removed if desired. An accompanying teacher's volume, the *Side by Side Activity & Test Prep Workbook 1 Teacher's Resource Book*, includes answer keys, scoring rubrics and guidelines, reproducible learner assessment records for documenting students' progress, teaching suggestions, and test preparation techniques.

Side by Side, 3rd edition
Activity & Test Prep Workbook 1

Copyright © 2001 by Prentice Hall Regents
Addison Wesley Longman, Inc.
A Pearson Education Company.
All rights reserved.
No part of this publication may be reproduced, stored in a retrieval system, or transmitted in any form or by any means, electronic, mechanical, photocopying, recording, or otherwise, without the prior permission of the publisher.

Pearson Education, 10 Bank Street, White Plains, NY 10606

Vice president, director of publishing: *Allen Ascher*
Editorial manager: *Pam Fishman*
Vice president, director of design and production: *Rhea Banker*
Associate director of electronic production: *Aliza Greenblatt*
Production manager: *Ray Keating*
Director of manufacturing: *Patrice Fraccio*
Digital layout specialist: *Wendy Wolf, Paula Williams*

Associate art director: *Elizabeth Carlson*
Interior design: *Elizabeth Carlson, Wendy Wolf*
Cover design: *Elizabeth Carlson, Monika Popowitz*
Photographer: *Paul Tañedo*

The authors gratefully acknowledge the contribution of Tina Carver in the development of the original *Side by Side* program.

ISBN 0-13-040647-3

1 2 3 4 5 6 7 8 9 10 – CRK – 05 04 03 02 01

Contents

A WHAT ARE THEY SAYING?

what's	is	my	from	name	phone number
where	are	your	I'm	address	

1. _____What's_____ your name?

My _____ is Janet Miller.

2. What's your _____?

_____ address _____ 456 Main Street.

3. What's _____ phone number?

My _____ _____ is 654-3960.

4. What's _____ name?

My _____ is Ken Green.

5. _____ your address?

My _____ is 15 Park Street.

6. What's your _____ number?

_____ phone _____ is 379-1029.

7. _____ _____ you from?

_____ _____ Detroit.

B NAME/ADDRESS/PHONE NUMBER

STUDENT IDENTIFICATION CARD

Name: Maria   Gonzalez
      First Name   Last Name

Address: 235 Main Street

            Bronx, New York

Phone
Number: 741-8906

> My name is Maria Gonzalez.
> My address is 235 Main Street.
> My phone number is 741-8906.

How about you? What's YOUR name, address, and phone number?

STUDENT IDENTIFICATION CARD

Name: _____
      First Name   Last Name

Address: _____

         _____

Phone
Number: _____

My name _____ ....

....

My _____ _____ ....

.... _____ ....

My _____ _____ _____ _____

....

C LISTENING

Listen and circle the number you hear.

1. (5) / 9
2. 3 / 7
3. 1 / 2
4. 6 / 3
5. 4 / 1
6. 3 / 6
7. 5 / 4
8. 8 / 2
9. 10 / 0
10. 5 / 9

D NUMBERS

zero	0
one	1
two	2
three	3
four	4
five	5
six	6
seven	7
eight	8
nine	9
ten	10

Write the number.

four ____4____

seven _____

one _____

eight _____

ten _____

two _____

nine _____

six _____

five _____

three _____

Write the word.

6 ____six____

2 _____

7 _____

3 _____

1 _____

8 _____

10 _____

4 _____

9 _____

5 _____

E LISTENING

Listen and write the missing numbers.

1.

What's your phone number?

My phone number is 389-793_2_.

2.

What's your telephone number?

My telephone number is 837-29___3.

3.

What's your apartment number?

My apartment number is ___-B.

4.

What's your address?

My address is ___ Main Street.

5.

What's your fax number?

My fax number is 654-___ ___15.

6.

What's your license number?

My license number is 26___3___9___.

F LISTENING

Listen and write the missing letters.

1. C-A-_R_-T-___-R

2. J-O-___-N-___-O-___

3. ___-E-R-___-L-___

4. A-N-D-E-___-S-___-N

5. ___-H-I-L-___-I-P

6. ___-A-R-___-I-N-E-___

G WHAT ARE THEY SAYING?

name	meet	you	Hi	Nice

A. Hello. My ____name____¹ is Dan Harris.

B. _____². I'm Susan Wilson.

   Nice to _____³ you.

A. _____⁴ to meet _____⁵, too.

is	you	Hello	I'm	My	to

A. Hi. _____⁶ name _____⁷ Alice Lane.

B. _____⁸. _____⁹ Bob Chang.

A. Nice _____¹⁰ meet you.

B. Nice to meet _____¹¹, too.

H GRAMMARRAP: Hi! Hello!

Listen. Then clap and practice.

A. Hi. I'm Jack.

B. Hello. I'm Jill.

C. Hi. I'm Mary.

D. Hello. I'm Bill.

All. Nice to meet you.

   Nice to meet you, too.

A. Hi. I'm Bob.

B. Hello. I'm Tim.

C. Hi. I'm Susie.

D. Hello. I'm Jim.

All. Nice to meet you.

   Nice to meet you, too.

A PUZZLE

Across

1.

5.

6.

8.

10.

12.

Down

1.

2.

3.

4.

7.

8.

9.

11.

B LISTENING

Listen and put a check (✓) under the correct picture.

1. ✔ _____   2. _____ _____   3. _____ _____

4. _____ _____   5. _____ _____   6. _____ _____

● **6**   Activity Workbook

C WHAT ARE THEY SAYING?

I'm	are	basement	attic	living room
we're	where	dining room	yard	bedroom
they're	you	kitchen	bathroom	

1. <u>Where</u> are you?

    <u>I'm</u> in the _____.

2. Where _____ Susan and Joe?

    _____ in the _____.

3. Where _____ you and Julie?

    _____ in the _____.

4. _____ are you?

    _____ in the _____.

5. _____ _____ Ben and Maria?

    _____ in the _____.

6. Where _____ you and Betty?

    _____ in the _____.

7. _____ _____ Pam and Peter?

    _____ in the _____.

8. _____ _____ you?

    _____ in the _____.

D WHAT ARE THEY SAYING?

where's	she's	classroom	garage	he's	living room	it's

1. ___Where's___ David?

   ___He's___ in the _____.

2. _____ Millie?

   _____ in the _____.

3. _____ the computer?

   _____ in the _____.

E WHERE ARE THEY?

we	he	they
	she	
	it	

(Mr. and Mrs. Chen)   1. _____They_____ are in the kitchen.

(Ms. Carter)   2. _____ is in the dining room.

(Mr. Grant)   3. _____ is in the bathroom.

(Harry and Mary)   4. _____ are in the basement.

(Ellen and I)   5. _____ are in the attic.

(The bookshelf)   6. _____ is in the living room.

(Mr. White)   7. _____ is in the garage.

(Mrs. Miller)   8. _____ is in the classroom.

(The telephone book)   9. _____ is in the bedroom.

F WHERE ARE THEY?

I'm	we're	he's	where's
	you're	she's	
	they're	it's	

(He is)   1. _____He's_____ in the bedroom.

(They are)   2. _____ in the basement.

(We are)   3. _____ in the attic.

(I am)   4. _____ in the bathroom.

(It is)   5. _____ in the dining room.

(She is)   6. _____ in the living room.

(You are)   7. _____ in the garage.

(Where is)   8. _____ the cell phone?

G THE BAKER FAMILY

The Baker family is at home today. **(1)** Mrs. Baker is __in__ __the__ __living__ __room__. **(2)** Mr. Baker is _____ _____ _____. **(3)** Peggy and Jim are _____ _____ _____. **(4)** Kevin is _____ _____ _____. **(5)** Susie is _____ _____ _____. **(6)** And the car is _____ _____ _____.

H WHERE ARE THEY?

he's	they're
she's	
it's	

1. Where's Mrs. Baker?   _She's in the living room._

2. Where's Mr. Baker?   _____

3. Where are Peggy and Jim?   _____

4. Where's Kevin?   _____

5. Where's Susie?   _____

6. Where's the car?   _____

1 WHAT'S THE SIGN?

Fill in the signs. Then complete the sentences.

1. Helen is _____ _in the park_ _____.

2. Mr. and Mrs. Grant are _____
_____.

3. Edward is _____.

4. Maria is _____.

5. Jim and Sarah are _____
_____.

6. Billy is _____.

7. The monkey is _____.

8. Ms. Johnson is _____.

Listen and write the number under the correct picture.

_____

___1___

_____

_____

_____

_____

K LISTENING

Listen and circle the word you hear.

1. zoo (you)   3. We're   They're   5. Where   Where's   7. on   in

2. Ms.   Mr.   4. Where   How   6. She's   He's   8. Is   It's

L MATCHING

Match the nationality and the city.

_c_ 1. We're Mexican. We're from _____.   a. Shanghai

___ 2. She's Greek. She's from _____.   b. San Juan

___ 3. He's Chinese. He's from _____.   c. Mexico City

___ 4. I'm Italian. I'm from_____.   d. Seoul

___ 5. They're Puerto Rican. They're from _____.   e. Athens

___ 6. We're Korean. We're from _____.   f. Tokyo

___ 7. She's Japanese. She's from _____.   g. Rome

M GRAMMARRAP: *Where's Jack?*

Listen. Then clap and practice.

A. Where's Jack?

B. He's in the kitchen.

A. Where's Jill?

B. She's in the dining room.

A. Where's Mom?

B. She's in the living room.

A. Where's Fred? Fred's in bed.

All. Fred's in bed.
Fred's in bed.

A. Jack's in the kitchen.

All. Fred's in bed.

A. Jack's in the kitchen.

B. Jill's in the dining room.

A. Mom's in the living room.

All. Fred's in bed.

N GRAMMARRAP: *Where Are Fred and Mary?*

Listen. Then clap and practice.

Where are	Fred and Mary

A. Where's Jack?

B. Where's Jill?

C. Where are Fred and Mary?

D. Where's Bill?

A. Where's Ed?

B. Where's Sue?

C. Where are Bob and Betty?

D. Where are Tom and Lou?

A. Jack and Jill.

B. Betty and Bill.

C. Bob and Lou.

D. Mary and Sue.

A. Jack and Jill.

B. Betty and Bill.

C. Bob and Lou.

D. Mary and Sue.

A WHAT ARE THEY SAYING?

doing	watching	I'm	we're	you
reading	sleeping	he's	they're	what
playing	eating	she's	are	what's
studying	cooking			

1. _____What_____ are you doing?

I'm _____ English.

2. What's Carla _____?

_____ _____.

3. _____ Walter doing?

_____.

4. _____ _____ Julie and David doing?

_____ _____ the newspaper.

5. _____ _____ you and George doing?

_____ _____ TV.

6. _____ _____ you _____?

_____ the piano.

7. _____ William doing?

_____ dinner.

B WHAT ARE THEY DOING?

cooking	eating	playing	singing	studying	watching
drinking	listening	reading	sleeping	teaching	

1. He's _____eating_____ breakfast.

2. She's _____ milk.

3. They're _____ mathematics.

4. He's _____ the newspaper.

5. They're _____ .

6. She's _____ .

7. He's _____ to music.

8. They're _____ TV.

9. She's _____ dinner.

10. He's _____ .

11. They're _____ baseball.

Listen and put a check (✓) under the correct picture.

1. ✔   _____

2. _____   _____

3. _____   _____

4. _____   _____

5. _____   _____

6. _____   _____

7. _____   _____

8. _____   _____

9. _____   _____

10. _____   _____

D **GRAMMARRAP:** *Frank?! At the Bank?!*

Listen. Then clap and practice.

A. Where's   Frank?

B. He's working at the   bank.

A.   Frank?!   At the bank?!

B.   Yes, that's   right.

He's working at the   bank.

All.   Frank?!   At the bank?!   Oh,   no!

A. Where's   Sue?

B. She's working at the   zoo.

A.   Sue?!   At the zoo?!

B.   Yes, that's   right.

She's working at the   zoo.

All.   Sue?!   At the zoo?!   Oh,   no!

A. Where's   Paul?

B. He's working at the   mall.

A.   Paul?!   At the mall?!

B.   Yes, that's   right.

He's working at the   mall.

All.   Paul?!   At the mall?!   Oh,   no!

E WHAT'S THE QUESTION?

Where is { he / she / it } ?	What's { he / she / it } doing?
Where are { you / they } ?	What are { you / they } doing?

1. __Where__ __are__ __you__ ?

2. __What's__ __he__ __doing__ ?

3. _____ _____ _____ ?

4. _____ _____ _____ _____ ?

5. _____ _____ _____ ?

6. _____ _____ _____ ?

7. _____ _____ _____ ?

8. _____ _____ _____ ?

9. _____ _____ _____ ?

10. _____ _____ _____ ?

11. _____ _____ _____ _____ ?

12. _____ _____ _____ ?

I'm in the garage

He's cooking dinner.

They're in the park.

We're playing with the dog.

He's in the attic.

She's listening to the radio.

She's in the yard.

We're at the beach.

He's sleeping.

It's in the classroom.

They're eating lunch.

I'm in the hospital.

F GRAMMARRAP: *Eating Lunch*

Listen. Then clap and practice.

What's he	Where are	What are

A. Where's   Charlie?

B.   He's in the   kitchen.

A. What's he   doing?

B.   Eating   lunch.

All.   Charlie's in the   kitchen   eating   lunch.

       Charlie's in the   kitchen   eating   lunch.

A. Who's in the   kitchen?

B.   Charlie's in the   kitchen.

A. What's he   doing?

B.   Eating   lunch.

A. Where's   Betty?

B.   She's in the   bedroom.

A. What's she   doing?

B.   Reading a   book.

18   **Activity Workbook**

All. Betty's in the   bedroom   reading a   book.

Betty's in the   bedroom   reading a   book.

A. Who's in the   bedroom?

B. Betty's in the   bedroom.

A. What's she   doing?

B. Reading a   book.

A. Where are Mom and   Dad?

B. They're in the   living room.

A. What are they   doing?

B. Watching Channel   Seven.

All. Betty's in the   bedroom.

Mom's in the   living room.

Dad's in the   living room.

Charlie's in the   kitchen.

A. Where's   Charlie?

All. He's in the   kitchen.

A. What's he   doing?

All. Eating   lunch.

✓ CHECK-UP TEST: Chapters 1-3

A. Answer the questions.

Ex. What's your telephone number?

My ....telephone number is 567-1032.....

1. What's your name?

   ....

2. What's your address?

   ....

3. Where are you from?

   ....

B. Circle the correct answer.

Ex. The map is on the [yard / (wall) / park] .

1. We're eating [milk / cards / lunch] .

2. [What / Where's / What's] Ben doing?

3. Max is [planting flowers / swimming / singing] in the bathroom.

4. Ms. Park is teaching [dinner / mathematics / the radio] .

5. Nice to [hello / hi / meet] you.

6. The [pencil / attic / shower] is in the classroom.

C. Fill in the blanks.

Ex. ___What's___ Bill doing?

1. Maria is _____ the hospital.

2. I'm _____ the newspaper.

3. Where's Joe? _____ in the cafeteria.

4. They're _____ TV.

5. What are you and Peter doing? _____ reading.

6. _____ the car? It's in the garage.

7. What are you _____? I'm studying.

8. Where's the cell phone? _____ in the basement.

9. _____ are Mr. and Mrs. Chen doing?

10. Carol _____ Bob are eating breakfast.

D. Listen and write the letter or number you hear.

Ex. M-A-R-_K_

1. C-A-R-___E-R

2. 354-9___12

3. 890-74___2

4. ___-U-L-I-E

5. 6___2-3059

6. 517___349

A WHAT ARE THEY DOING?

what	my	our	cleaning	apartment
what's	his	their	doing	children
are	her		fixing	homework
				sink

1. Hi! __What's__ Jason doing?

   He's _____ _____ room.

2. What's Peggy _____?

   She's _____ _____ car.

3. _____ are you doing?

   I'm cleaning _____ _____.

4. What are your _____ doing?

   They're doing _____ _____.

5. What _____ you doing?

   We're fixing _____ _____.

Activity Workbook   **21**

B WHAT'S THE WORD?

| my | his | her | its | our | your | their |

1. I'm feeding ____my____ cat.

2. We're washing _____ clothes.

3. They're painting _____ bedroom.

4. She's fixing _____ sink.

5. It's eating _____ dinner.

6. You're cleaning _____ yard.

7. He's reading _____ e-mail.

C LISTENING

Listen and circle the word you hear.

1. your   (our)   3. her   his   5. your   our

2. his   her   4. our   their   6. my   its

D PUZZLE

Across

1. I'm painting _____ apartment.

3. We're fixing _____ TV.

6. Bobby and Tim are cleaning _____ room.

7. Bill is doing _____ homework.

Down

2. You're doing _____ exercises.

4. The dog is eating _____ dinner.

5. Ruth is brushing _____ teeth.

E WHAT ARE THEY SAYING?

| Yes, I am. | Yes, { he / she / it } is. | Yes, { we / you / they } are. |

1. A. Is Harry feeding his cat?

   B. <u>Yes, he is.</u>

2. A. Are you and Tom cleaning your yard?

   B. _____ _____ _____

3. A. Is Mrs. Chen doing her exercises?

   B. _____ _____ _____

4. A. Are your children brushing their teeth?

   B. _____ _____ _____

5. A. Is George sleeping?

   B. _____ _____ _____

6. A. Is Irene planting flowers?

   B. _____ _____ _____

7. A. Are you washing your windows?

   B. _____ _____ _____

8. A. Am I in the hospital?

   B. _____ _____ _____

F **GRAMMARRAP:** *Busy! Busy! Busy!*

Listen. Then clap and practice.

What are	Is he	Yes, he	What's he

A. Are you busy?

B. Yes, I   am.

A. What are you   doing?

B. I'm talking to   Sam.

A. Is he busy?

B. Yes, he   is.

A. What's he   doing?

B. He's talking to   Liz.

A. Are they busy?

B. Yes, they   are.

A. What are they   doing?

B. They're washing their   car.

All.   I'm talking to   Sam.

He's talking to   Liz.

They're washing their   car.

They're busy!

G **LISTENING**

Listen and circle the word you hear.

1. (he's)   she's   3. feeding   eating   5. our   their

2. his   her   4. apartment   yard   6. washing   watching

H WHAT ARE THEY DOING?

1. He's _____washing_____ his hair.

2. They're _____ their yard.

3. We're _____ our exercises.

4. I'm _____ my e-mail.

5. She's _____ her living room.

6. You're _____ your cat.

I WHAT'S THE WORD?

Circle the correct words.

1. (They're) / Their washing they're / their windows.

2. Where / We're are Mr. and Mrs. Tanaka?

3. He's / His doing he's / his exercises.

4. Where are / Where's the cell phone?

5. We're brushing are / our teeth.

6. His / Is Richard busy?

7. What are / our you doing?

8. The cat is eating it's / its dinner.

laundromat	doing	playing	they're	what's	her	are
library	eating	reading	he's	where's	their	and
park	fixing	washing	she's	in	his	
restaurant	listening					

Everybody is busy today. Ms. Roberts is in the ___restaurant___ 1. She's _____ 2

dinner. Mr. and Mrs. Lopez are _____ 3 the health club. _____ 4 doing _____ 5

exercises. Patty and Danny Williams are in the _____ 6. She's _____ 7 the

newspaper. He's _____ 8 to music. Mr. _____ 9 Mrs. Sharp are also in the park.

What are they _____ 10? They're _____ 11 cards.

Jenny Chang is in the _____ 12. _____ 13 washing _____ 14 clothes.

Charlie Harris and Julie Carter _____ 15 in the parking lot. He's _____ 16

_____ 17 car. She's _____ 18 her bicycle. _____ 19 Mr. Molina? He's in the

_____ 20. _____ 21 he doing? _____ 22 reading a book.

A MATCHING OPPOSITES

_d_ 1. large   **a.** thin

___ 2. heavy   **b.** rich

___ 3. single   **c.** beautiful

___ 4. ugly   **d.** small

___ 5. cheap   **e.** young

___ 6. poor   **f.** expensive

___ 7. old   **g.** married

___ 8. tall   **h.** heavy

___ 9. difficult   **i.** old

___ 10. new   **j.** ugly

___ 11. handsome   **k.** big

___ 12. thin   **l.** easy

___ 13. little   **m.** noisy

___ 14. quiet   **n.** short

B WHAT ARE THEY SAYING?

Tell me about your new friend.

1. Is he short or _____ tall _____?

2. Is he heavy or _____?

3. Is he old or _____?

4. Is he single or _____?

Tell me about the apartment.

5. Is it large or _____?

6. Is it quiet or _____?

7. Is it cheap or _____?

8. Is it beautiful or _____?

C LISTENING

Listen and circle the word you hear.

1. small   (tall)   3. easy   noisy   5. ugly   young

2. ugly   heavy   4. thin   single   6. cheap   easy

D WHAT'S WRONG?

He She It } isn't	They aren't

1. It's new.

   _____It isn't new._____

   _____It's old._____

2. They're quiet.

   _____

   _____

3. It's large.

   _____

   _____

4. He's single.

   _____

   _____

5. She's young.

   _____

   _____

6. They're short.

   _____

   _____

E SCRAMBLED QUESTIONS

Unscramble the questions. Begin each question with a capital letter.

1. _____Are you busy_____?
   busy   you   are

2. _____?
   dog   your   large   is

3. _____?
   they   are   married

4. _____?
   I   beautiful   am

5. _____?
   difficult   English   is

6. _____?
   new   is   car   their

7. _____?
   tall   she   is   short   or

8. _____?
   noisy   quiet   he   is   or

GrammarRap: *Old! Cold! Tall! Small!*

Listen. Then clap and practice.

All.	Is he	young?	*(clap) (clap)*
	Is he	old?	*(clap) (clap)*
	Is it	hot?	*(clap) (clap)*
	Is it	cold?	*(clap) (clap)*
	Is she	short?	*(clap) (clap)*
	Is she	tall?	*(clap) (clap)*
	Is it	large?	*(clap) (clap)*
	Is it	small?	*(clap) (clap)*
		Young!	Old!
		Hot!	Cold!
		Young!	Old!
		Hot!	Cold!

A.	Is he young or	old?
B.	He's very	old.
A.	Is it hot or	cold?
B.	It's very	cold.

A.	Is she short or	tall?
B.	She's very	tall.
A.	Is it large or	small?
B.	It's extremely	small.

All.	Young!	Old!
	Hot!	Cold!
	Short!	Tall!
	Large!	Small!

G WHOSE THINGS?

| bicycle | book | car | cat | computer | dog | guitar | house | piano | TV |

1. ___Albert's___ ___car___

2. _____

3. _____

4. _____

5. _____

6. _____

7. _____

8. _____

9. _____

10. _____

H WHAT'S THE WORD?

His	Her	Their	Its

1. Mary's brother isn't short.   (His (Her)) brother is tall.
2. Mr. and Mrs. Miller's apartment isn't cheap.   (His   Their) apartment is expensive.
3. Robert's sister isn't single.   (His   Her) sister is married.
4. Ms. Clark's neighbors aren't quiet.   (Their   Her) neighbors are noisy.
5. Their dog's name isn't Rover.   (Its   Their) name is Fido.
6. Mrs. Hunter's car isn't large.   (His   Her) car is small.
7. Timmy's bicycle isn't new.   (His   Its) bicycle is old.
8. Mr. and Mrs. Lee's son isn't single. (Her   Their) son is married.

I MR. AND MRS. GRANT

Read the story and answer the questions.

I		am.
Yes,	he / she / it	is.
	we / you / they	are.

I'm		not.
No,	he / she / it	isn't.
	we / you / they	aren't.

Meet Mr. and Mrs. Grant. Mr. Grant is short and heavy. Mrs. Grant is tall and thin. Their house is small and old. Their car is new and expensive. Their neighbors are noisy. And their cat is ugly.

1. Is Mr. Grant short? ___Yes, he is.___
2. Is he tall? _____
3. Is he thin? _____
4. Is he heavy? _____
5. Is Mrs. Grant tall? _____
6. Is she heavy? _____
7. Is she thin? _____

8. Is their house large? _____
9. Is it old? _____
10. Is their car new? _____
11. Is it cheap? _____
12. Are their neighbors quiet? _____
13. Are they noisy? _____
14. Is their cat pretty? _____

J HOW'S THE WEATHER?

it's sunny	it's raining	it's warm	it's hot
it's cloudy	it's snowing	it's cool	it's cold

Weather Around the World

Mexico City
Miami
New York
Rome
San Francisco
San Juan
Seoul
Tokyo

1. How's the weather in Mexico City?   <u>It's</u> <u>   warm.   </u>

2. How's the weather in Miami?   _____ _____

3. How's the weather in New York?   _____ _____

4. How's the weather in Rome?   _____ _____

5. How's the weather in San Francisco?   _____ _____

6. How's the weather in San Juan?   _____ _____

7. How's the weather in Seoul?   _____ _____

8. How's the weather in Tokyo?   _____ _____

9. How's the weather in YOUR city?   ....

K LISTENING

Listen and circle the word you hear.

1. cold	(cool)	3. sunny	snowing	5. raining	snowing
2. snowing	sunny	4. cool	hot	6. sunny	cloudy

Numbers

0	zero	10	ten	20	twenty	30	thirty
1	one	11	eleven	21	twenty-one	40	forty
2	two	12	twelve	22	twenty-two	50	fifty
3	three	13	thirteen	23	twenty-three	60	sixty
4	four	14	fourteen	24	twenty-four	70	seventy
5	five	15	fifteen	25	twenty-five	80	eighty
6	six	16	sixteen	26	twenty-six	90	ninety
7	seven	17	seventeen	27	twenty-seven	100	one hundred
8	eight	18	eighteen	28	twenty-eight		
9	nine	19	nineteen	29	twenty-nine		

L WHAT'S THE NUMBER?

1. twenty-four   _24_
2. thirty-one   _____
3. seventy-two   _____
4. forty-six   _____
5. ninety-seven   _____

M WHAT'S THE WORD?

38   _thirty-eight_
83   _____
55   _____
99   _____
64   _____

N NUMBER PUZZLE

Across

2. 46
5. 29
8. 8
9. 0
10. 11
11. 50

Down

1. 60
3. 15
4. 7
5. 20
6. 12
7. 90

O LISTENING

Listen to the temperature in Fahrenheit and Celsius. Write the numbers you hear.

1. Los Angeles _86°_ F/ _30°_ C
2. Seoul _____ F/ _____ C
3. San Juan _____ F/ _____ C
4. Hong Kong _____ F/ _____ C

5. Miami _____ F/ _____ C
6. London _____ F/ _____ C
7. Mexico City _____ F/ _____ C
8. Moscow _____ F/ _____ C

P GRAMMARRAP: *Terrible Weather! Beautiful Weather!*

Listen. Then clap and practice.

It's raining in   Alaska.
It's snowing in   L.A.
It's cloudy in   Caracas.
It's TERRIBLE   today!

It's warm in   Pennsylvania.
It's sunny in   Bombay.
It's cool in   Guatemala.
It's BEAUTIFUL   today!

Q MATCHING

Match the questions and answers.

_e_ 1. Is your brother tall?

___ 2. Is your computer new?

___ 3. Is it hot today?

___ 4. Hi! Are you busy?

___ 5. Are your neighbors quiet?

___ 6. Is she young?

___ 7. Is her husband heavy?

___ 8. Is your sister married?

___ 9. Are these questions difficult?

a. Yes, I am. I'm studying.

b. No, she isn't. She's single.

c. No, she isn't. She's old.

d. No, it isn't. It's cold.

e. No, he isn't. He's short.

f. No, he isn't. He's thin.

g. No, they aren't. They're easy.

h. No, it isn't. It's old.

i. No, they aren't. They're noisy.

brother	sister
children	son
daughter	wife
husband	

father	grandmother
grandchildren	grandparents
granddaughter	grandson
grandfather	mother

Bill and Jane are married. Jane is Bill's _____wife_____ [1] . Bill is Jane's _____ [2] .

Timmy and Sally are their _____ [3] . Timmy is their _____ [4], and Sally is their

_____ [5] . Timmy is Sally's _____ [6], and Sally is Timmy's _____ [7] .

Walter and Helen are Jane's parents. Walter is Jane's _____ [8], and Helen is Jane's

_____ [9] . Walter and Helen are Timmy and Sally's _____ [10] . Walter is

their _____ [11], and Helen is their _____ [12] . Timmy and Sally are

Walter and Helen's _____ [13] . Timmy is their _____ [14], and Sally

is their _____ [15] .

aunt	nephew	uncle
cousin	niece	

John is Jane's brother. Judy is John's wife.

Danny is their son. John is Timmy and Sally's

_____ [16], and Judy is their _____ [17].

Timmy is John and Judy's _____ [18],

and Sally is their _____ [19]. Danny is

Timmy and Sally's _____ [20].

LISTENING

Listen and put a check (✓) under the correct picture.

1.   ✔   _____   2.   _____   _____

3.   _____   _____   4.   _____   _____

5.   _____   _____   6.   _____   _____

7.   _____   _____   8.   _____   _____

C   **THE WRONG WORD!**

Put a circle around the wrong word.

1.	large	small	(cheap)	little	6.	rugs	parents	cousins	children
2.	kitchen	bathroom	bedroom	park	7.	pencil	book	pen	bank
3.	guitar	baseball	drums	piano	8.	Miss	Mr.	Ms.	Mrs.
4.	handsome	beautiful	tall	pretty	9.	quiet	noisy	poor	loud
5.	hot	dinner	warm	cool	10.	son	sister	nephew	brother

Listen and fill in the words to the song. Then listen again and sing along.

| crying | dancing | hanging | having | living | looking | smiling | working |

I'm looking at the photographs.

They're hanging in the hall.

I'm _____smiling_____ 1 at the memories,

looking at the pictures on the wall.

My son Robert's married now.

I'm _____ 2 in L.A. (Hi, Dad!)

My daughter's _____ 3 in Detroit.

I'm very far away. (I love you, Dad!)

I'm _____ 4 at the photographs.

They're _____ 5 in the hall.

I'm smiling at the memories,

looking at the pictures on the wall.

My mom and dad are _____ 6.

It's a very special day.

(We're _____ 7 a good time!)

My little sister's _____ 8.

It's my brother's wedding day.
(I'm so happy!)

I'm _____ 9 at the photographs.

They're _____ 10 in the hall.

I'm _____ 11 at the memories,

_____ 12 at the pictures on the wall.

I'm smiling at the memories,

looking at the pictures on the wall.

AN E-MAIL FROM LOS ANGELES

```
                                                            ▲
        To: alex@ttm.com
        From: bob@aal.com

     Dear Alex,

        Our new home in Los Angeles is large and pretty.  Los Angeles is
     beautiful.  The weather is warm and sunny.  Today it's 78˚F.

        Our family is in the park today, and we're having a good time.  My
     mother is reading a book, and my father is listening to music.  My sister
     Patty is riding her bicycle, and my brother Tom is skateboarding.

        My grandparents aren't in the park today.  They're at home.  My
     grandmother is baking, and my grandfather is planting flowers
     in the yard.

        How's the weather in New York today?  Is it snowing?  What are
     you and your family doing?
                                                            ▼
```

Answer these questions in complete sentences.

1. Where is Bob's new home? _____It's in Los Angeles._____

2. How's the weather in Los Angeles? _____

3. What's the temperature? _____

4. Where are Bob and his family today? _____

5. What's Bob's mother doing? _____

6. What's his father doing? _____

7. Who is Patty? _____

8. What's she doing? _____

9. Who is Tom? _____

10. What's he doing? _____

11. Are Bob's grandparents in the park? _____

12. Where are they? _____

13. What's his grandmother doing? _____

14. What's his grandfather doing? _____

15. Is Alex in Los Angeles? _____

16. Where is he? _____

F GRAMMARRAP: *No. She's in Spain.*

Listen. Then clap and practice.

A.   What's Jack   doing?
B.   He's working in   Rome.
A. What's BOB   doing?
B.   He's working at   HOME.

A.   Is Jack at   home?
B.   No. HE'S in   ROME.
A.   Is BOB in   Rome?
B.   No. HE'S at   HOME.

All.   Jack's in   Rome.

     Jack's in   Rome.

What's BOB   doing?

     He's working at   HOME.

A.   What's Jane   doing?
B.   She's working in   Spain.
A. What's MARY   doing?
B.   She's working in   MAINE.

A.   Is Jane in   Maine?
B.   No. SHE'S in   SPAIN.
A.   Is Mary in   Spain?
B.   No. SHE'S in   MAINE.

All.   Jane's in   Spain.

     Jane's in   Spain.

What's MARY   doing?

     She's working in   MAINE.

✓ CHECK-UP TEST: Chapters 4-6

A. Circle the correct answers.

Ex. Jack is sitting on his [computer / TV / (bicycle)] .

1. He's my [nephew / wife / sister] .

2. We're standing [on / at / in] front of our house.

3. They're swimming at the [yard / kitchen / beach] .

4. He's feeding the dog [its / it's / he] dinner.

5. He's sleeping [at / on / in] the sofa.

6. Mrs. Kent is [raining / feeding / reading] in the park.

7. We're [fixing / snowing / riding] our car.

8. They're [painting / eating / brushing] their teeth.

B. Fill in the blanks.

Ex. _____What's_____ his name?

1. _____ are they? They're in Tahiti.

2. My mother's mother is my _____.

3. My sister's daughter is my _____.

4. _____ is he? He's my cousin.

5. Mr. Jones is playing a game on _____ computer.

6. My children are doing _____ homework.

7. Ms. Kim is busy. She's fixing _____ sink.

C. Write a sentence with the opposite adjective.

Ex. Their car isn't cheap. _____It's expensive._____

1. My brother isn't heavy. _____

2. They aren't short. _____

3. My computer isn't old. _____

D. Write the question.

Ex. ___Is it ugly?___ No, it isn't. It's beautiful.

1. _____ No, I'm not. I'm single.

2. _____ No, she isn't. She's old.

3. _____ No, they aren't. They're noisy.

E. Listen and choose the correct response.

Ex. No, he isn't. (a.) He's young.   b. He's thin.

1. No, it isn't.   a. It's difficult.   b. It's small.
2. No, she isn't.   a. She's rich.   b. She's short.
3. No, it isn't.   a. It's easy.   b. It's cloudy.
4. No, he isn't.   a. He's tall.   b. He's loud.

A WHERE IS IT?

across from	around the corner from	next to	between

1. The bank is _____next to_____ the restaurant.

2. The bus station is _____ the fire station.

3. The library is _____ the movie theater and the barber shop.

4. The laundromat is _____ the video store.

5. The laundromat is _____ the clinic.

6. The clinic is _____ the laundromat and the gas station.

7. The clinic and the gas station are _____ the hotel.

8. The barber shop is _____ the post office.

9. The restaurant is _____ the supermarket.

10. The school is _____ the supermarket and the hotel.

11. The school is _____ the laundromat.

Activity Workbook   41

WHAT ARE THEY SAYING?

Is there	There's	across from	around the corner from
there		between	next to

1. Excuse me. Is there a bank in this neighborhood?

    Yes, there is. _____There's_____ a bank on Park Street, _____next to_____ the school.

2. Excuse me. _____ a video store in this neighborhood?

    Yes, there is. _____ a video store on Main Street, _____ the clinic.

3. Excuse me. Is there a supermarket in this neighborhood?

    Yes, _____ is. _____ a supermarket on School Street, _____ the post office.

4. Excuse me. _____ a park in this neighborhood?

    Yes, there is. _____ a park on State Street, _____ the drug store and the library.

5. Excuse me. _____ a gas station in this neighborhood?

    Yes, _____ is. _____ a gas station on _____ Avenue, _____ the fire station.

Listen to the sentences about the buildings on the map. After each sentence, write the name on the correct building.

1. bakery	4. library	7. hair salon	10. park
2. school	5. hospital	8. supermarket	11. health club
3. department store	6. police station	9. video store	12. train station

D YES OR NO?

Look at the map and answer the questions.

1. Is there a fire station on Oak Street?   Yes, there is.   No, there isn't.

2. Is there a hair salon across from the barber shop?   Yes, there is.   No, there isn't.

3. Is there a supermarket around the corner from the bank?   Yes, there is.   No, there isn't.

4. Is there a police station next to the hospital?   Yes, there is.   No, there isn't.

5. Is there a department store across from the school?   Yes, there is.   No, there isn't.

6. Is there a drug store on Oak Street?   Yes, there is.   No, there isn't.

7. Is there a laundromat next to the park?   Yes, there is.   No, there isn't.

8. Is there a church on River Avenue?   Yes, there is.   No, there isn't.

9. Is there a bank between the barber shop and the bakery?   Yes, there is.   No, there isn't.

Activity Workbook   **43**

Listen. Then clap and practice.

| | | SUPERMARKET | RESTAURANT | LAUNDROMAT | |

All. There's a nice big   supermarket   just around the   corner.

There's a good cheap   restaurant   just around the   corner.

There's a nice clean   laundromat   just around the   corner.

There's a quiet little   park   just around the   corner.

Just around the   corner?   Thanks   very much.

A. Is there a nice big   supermarket   anywhere   around here?

B. Yes, there   is.   Yes, there   is.

There's a nice big   supermarket   just around the   corner.

A. Just around the   corner?   Thanks very   much.

A. Is there a good cheap   restaurant   anywhere   around here?

B. Yes, there   is.   Yes, there   is.

There's a good cheap   restaurant   just around the   corner.

A. Just around the   corner?   Thanks very   much.

A. Is there a nice clean   laundromat   anywhere   around here?

B. Yes, there   is.   Yes, there   is.

There's a nice clean   laundromat   just around the   corner.

A. Just around the   corner?   Thanks very   much.

A. Is there a quiet little   park   anywhere   around here?

B. Yes, there   is.   Yes, there   is.

There's a quiet little   park   just around the   corner.

A. Just around the   corner?   Thanks very   much.

WHAT ARE THEY SAYING?

is there	there is	there isn't	there are
are there	there's		there aren't

1. _____Is_____ _____there_____ an elevator in the building?

2. Yes, _____ _____.

3. How many closets _____ _____ in the apartment?

4. _____ a large closet in the bedroom, and _____ _____ two small closets in the living room.

5. _____ _____ a jacuzzi in the bathroom?

6. No, _____ _____. But _____ _____ two air conditioners in the apartment.

7. _____ _____ any washing machines in the building?

8. No, _____ _____. But _____ a laundromat across the street.

9. How many windows _____ _____ in the apartment?

10. _____ _____ three windows in the living room, and _____ one window in the bedroom.

broken	closets	escape	machines	satellite dish	mice
cats	dogs	hole	mailbox	refrigerator	stop

1. There aren't any washing _____machines_____ in the basement.

2. There's a _____ window in the bathroom.

3. There are _____ in the basement.

4. There isn't a fire _____.

5. There's a _____ in the wall in the living room.

6. There's a _____ on the roof.

7. There's a _____ in the kitchen.

8. There are two _____ in the bedroom.

9. There aren't any _____ in the building, but there are _____.

10. There isn't a bus _____ outside the building, but there's a _____.

Yes, there is. No, there isn't.	Yes, there are. No, there aren't.

1. Is there a computer in Jane's living room?

   _____Yes, there is._____

2. Is there a desk in the living room?

   _____

3. Are there any flowers in the living room?

   _____

4. Is there a newspaper on the table?

   _____

5. Are there any photographs on the table?

   _____

6. Are there any clothes in the closet?

   _____

7. Are there any windows in the living room?

   _____

8. Is there a cat in the living room?

   _____

9. Are there any chairs in front of the windows?

   _____

10. Is there a bookshelf in the living room?

    _____

11. Is there a cell phone next to the computer?

    _____

12. Is there a television next to the bookshelf?

    _____

13. Are there any books on the sofa?

    _____

14. Is there a guitar on the chair?

    _____

I LOOKING FOR AN APARTMENT

a/c. = air conditioner	beaut. = beautiful	frpl(s). = fireplace(s)	nr. = near
apt. = apartment	bldg. = building	kit. = kitchen	rm(s). = room(s)
bath(s). = bathroom(s)	dinrm. = dining room	lge. = large	schl. = school
bdrm(s). = bedroom(s)	elev. = elevator	livrm. = living room	

www.UShomes.com **CHICAGO**

Quiet, sunny apt., kit., livrm., bdrm., bath., 2 frpls., no children, $900. 800-874-5555.

1. The apartment is in ____Chicago____.

2. It's quiet and _____.

3. There's a kitchen, a living room, a _____, and a _____.

4. There are two _____ in the apartment.

5. There aren't any _____ in the building.

www.UShomes.com **MIAMI**

Beaut. new apt., kit., livrm., 3 bdrms., 2 baths., elev. in building., $1200. 800-874-5555.

6. The apartment is in _____.

7. It's _____ and new.

8. There are three _____ in the apartment.

9. There are _____ bathrooms.

10. There's an _____ in the building.

www.UShomes.com **NEW YORK**

Sunny, lge. apt., kit., livrm., bdrm., bath., 2 a/c., nr. schl. $1800. 800-874-5555.

11. The apartment is in _____.

12. It's sunny and _____.

13. There's a kitchen, a _____, a bedroom, and a bathroom.

14. There are two _____.

15. The apartment is near a _____.

www.UShomes.com **DALLAS**

Lge. quiet apt., kit., livrm., dinrm., 2 bdrms., 2 baths., elev. in bldg., nr. bus. $850. 800-874-5555.

16. The apartment is in _____.

17. It's large and _____.

18. There's a _____, a kitchen, and a living room.

19. There's an elevator in the _____.

20. The apartment is _____ a bus stop.

J **GRAMMARRAP:** *Tell Me About the Apartment*

Listen. Then clap and practice.

There are

A.	Tell me about the apartment on	Elm Street.
B.	It's nice, but it	isn't very	cheap.
	There's a brand new	stove in the	kitchen.
	There's a beautiful	carpet on the	floor.
	There are three large	windows in the	living room.
	And the bedroom has a	sliding glass	door.
All.	The bedroom has a	sliding glass	door?!
B.	Yes, the bedroom has a	sliding glass	door.

A.	Tell me about the apartment on	Main Street.
B.	It's cheap, but it	isn't very	nice.
	There isn't a	tub in the	bathroom.
	There aren't any	lights in the	hall.
	There's a broken	window in the	dining room.
	And there are ten big	holes in the	wall!
All.	There are ten big	holes in the	wall?!
B.	Yes, there are ten big	holes in the	wall.

belt	briefcase	glasses	jeans	purse	sock	tie
blouse	coat	glove	mitten	shirt	stocking	umbrella
boots	dress	hat	necklace	shoe	suit	watch
bracelet	earring	jacket	pants	skirt	sweater	

1. _____tie_____
2. _____
3. _____
4. _____
5. _____

6. _____
7. _____
8. _____
9. _____
10. _____

11. _____
12. _____
13. _____
14. _____
15. _____

16. _____
17. _____
18. _____
19. _____

20. _____
21. _____
22. _____
23. _____

24. _____
25. _____
26. _____
27. _____

B A OR AN?

1. __a__ bus station
2. __an__ umbrella
3. _____ school
4. _____ office
5. _____ radio
6. _____ earring

7. _____ hospital
8. _____ antenna
9. _____ e-mail
10. _____ yard
11. _____ library
12. _____ cell phone

13. _____ exercise
14. _____ house
15. _____ bank
16. _____ woman
17. _____ apartment
18. _____ laundromat

19. _____ uncle
20. _____ attic
21. _____ flower
22. _____ aunt
23. _____ fax
24. _____ hotel

C SINGULAR/PLURAL

1. _____a hat_____   hats
2. _____   basements
3. a dress   _____
4. a boss   _____
5. an exercise   _____
6. _____   watches
7. _____   gloves
8. a sock   _____
9. a drum   _____

10. _____   rooms
11. an earring   _____
12. _____   purses
13. a niece   _____
14. a woman   _____
15. _____   children
16. a mouse   _____
17. _____   teeth
18. _____   people

D LISTENING

Listen and circle the word you hear.

1. umbrella   (umbrellas)
2. blouse   blouses
3. coat   coats
4. computer   computers
5. shoe   shoes
6. exercise   exercises
7. dress   dresses
8. restaurant   restaurants

9. necklace   necklaces
10. earring   earrings
11. belt   belts
12. watch   watches
13. niece   nieces
14. nephew   nephews
15. shirt   shirts
16. tie   ties

LISTENING

Listen and circle the color you hear.

1.	(blue)	black	3.	gray	gold	5.	purple	yellow
2.	red	green	4.	pink	silver	6.	orange	brown

F **COLORS**

Write sentences about yourself, using colors.

black	gray	pink	silver
blue	green	purple	white
brown	orange	red	yellow
gold			

1. My house/apartment is. . . . .

2. My bedroom is . . . .

3. My kitchen is . . . .

4. My bathroom is . . . .

5. My living room is . . . .

6. My classroom is . . . .

7. My English book is . . . .

8. My pencils are . . . .

9. My notebook is . . . .

10. My desk is . . . .

11. My shirt/blouse is. . . . .

12. My watch is . . . .

13. My socks/stockings are . . . .

14. My coat is . . . .

15. My hat is . . . .

16. My jeans are . . . .

17. My shoes are . . . .

18. My . . . . (is/are) . . . .

19. My . . . . (is/are) . . . .

20. My . . . . (is/are) . . . .

21. My . . . . (is/are) . . . .

22. My . . . . (is/are) . . . .

23. My . . . . (is/are) . . . .

24. My . . . . (is/are) . . . .

1. Yes, please. I'm looking for

   _____ a pair of pants _____ .

2. Yes, please. I'm looking for

   _____ .

3. Yes, please. I'm looking for

   _____ .

4. Yes, please. I'm looking for

   _____ .

5. Yes, please. I'm looking for

   _____ .

6. Yes, please. I'm looking for

   _____ .

7. Yes, please. I'm looking for

   _____ .

8. Yes, please. I'm looking for

   _____ .

9. Yes, please. I'm looking for

   _____ .

LISTENING

Listen and put a check (✓) under the correct picture.

1. _____   ___✔___   2. _____   _____

3. _____   _____   4. _____   _____

5. _____   _____   6. _____   _____

7. _____   _____   8. _____   _____

I **LISTENING**

Listen and circle the correct word to complete the sentence.

1. (is) red.
   are

2. is easy.
   are

3. is large.
   are

4. is gold.
   are

5. is beautiful.
   are

6. is new.
   are

7. is expensive.
   are

8. is small.
   are

9. is big.
   are

J THIS /THAT /THESE /THOSE

 this these   that those

  orange

1. _This hat is orange._

 yellow

2. _That hat is yellow._

 brown

3. _____

 black

4. _____

 expensive

5. _____

 cheap

6. _____

  small

7. _____

 large

8. _____

  pretty

9. _____

 ugly

10. _____

  gold

11. _____

 silver

12. _____

Activity Workbook   **55**

K SINGULAR → PLURAL

Write the sentence in the plural.

1. That coat is blue. _____ Those coats are blue. _____

2. This bracelet is new. _____

3. That watch is beautiful. _____

4. This is Tom's jacket. _____

5. This isn't your shoe. _____

6. Is that your earring? _____

7. That isn't your notebook. _____

8. This person isn't rich. _____

L PLURAL → SINGULAR

Write the sentence in the singular.

1. These sweaters are pretty. _____ This sweater is pretty. _____

2. Those purses are expensive. _____

3. Are these your neighbors? _____

4. Are those your dresses? _____

5. Those are Bill's shirts. _____

6. These women are my friends. _____

7. These aren't my gloves. _____

8. Those are her cats. _____

M SCRAMBLED SENTENCES

Unscramble the sentences. Begin each sentence with a capital letter.

1. ___ I think that's my jacket. ___
   jacket I that's think my

2. _____
   my these gloves new are

3. _____
   boots aren't those black your

4. _____
   year blue very this suits popular are

5. _____
   of here's nice sunglasses pair a

6. _____
   old that's car brother's my

N GRAMMARRAP: *Clothes In My Closet*

Listen. Then clap and practice.

This shirt is	red.		Old	red	shirt!
That skirt is	blue.		New	blue	skirt!
This shirt is	old.		Old	red	shirt!
That skirt is	new.		New	blue	skirt!

These suits are	silver.		New	silver	suits!
Those boots are	gold.		Old	gold	boots!
These suits are	new.		New	silver	suits!
Those boots are	old.		Old	gold	boots!

O GRAMMARRAP: *Black Leather Jacket*

Listen. Then clap and practice.

Blue	jeans,	gray	pants,
Black	leather	jacket!	
Blue	jeans,	gray	pants,
Black	leather	jacket!	
White	shirt,	silver	boots,
Black	leather	jacket!	
White	shirt,	silver	boots,
Black	leather	jacket!	
Cool	blue	jeans!	
Nice	gray	pants!	
White	shirt,	silver	boots,
Black	leather	jacket!	

| this | that |
| these | those |

1. _____This_____ is my favorite pair of jeans.

_____ are my new sweaters, and

_____ is my new coat.

2. _____That_____ 's a pretty coat.

Are _____ your new boots?

3. _____ is my classroom.

_____ is the bulletin board, and

_____ are the computers.

4. Are _____ your books, and

is _____ your pencil?

5. _____ is my favorite photograph.

_____ is my mother, and

_____ are my sisters and

brothers.

6. Are _____ your cousins?

Who's _____ handsome man?

GRAMMARSONG: *At the Laundromat*

Listen and fill in the words to the song. Then listen again and sing along.

hat	those	shirt	suits	that	are	skirt	that's	boots	these	this

Is _____this_____ [1] your sweater?

Is _____ [2] your _____ [3] ?

_____ [4] my blue jacket.

That's my pink _____ [5] .

I think _____ [6] is my new _____ [7] .

We're looking for _____ [8] and _____ [9] .

We're washing all our clothes at the laundromat.

_____ [10] and that. At the laundromat.

This and _____ [11] . At the laundromat.

_____ [12] and _____ [13] . At the laundromat.

Are _____ [14] your mittens?

_____ [15] these your _____ [16] ?

_____ [17] are my socks.

Those are my bathing _____ [18] .

Where _____ [19] my pantyhose?

We're looking for _____ [20] and _____ [21] .

We're washing all our clothes at the laundromat.

_____ [22] and _____ [23] .

Washing all our clothes.

_____ [24] and _____ [25] .

At the laundromat. At the laundromat.

(Hey! Give me _____ [26] !)

At the laundromat!

A. Circle the correct answers.

Ex.   My favorite color is 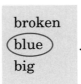 .

1.   Are | these / this / that | your children?

2.   Here's a nice pair | to / on / of | stockings.

3. | Are there / Is there / There | a jacuzzi in the apartment?

4.   There's an | earring / sweater / umbrellas | on the table.

5. | Who / What / How | many windows are there in the living room?

6.   There aren't any | man / people / hole | in the room.

7.   Dresses are over | there / their / they're | .

8.   Is there a stove in the kitchen?

> No, there aren't.
> No, they isn't.
> No, there isn't.

B. Answer the questions.

Ex.   Where's the book store?

It's next to the bank.

1.   Where's the bakery?

_____

2.   Where's the hospital?

_____

3.   Where's the video store?

_____

C. Circle the word that doesn't belong.

Ex. cotton   wool   vinyl   (cheap)

1. this   those   their   these

2. orange   striped   gray   pink

3. closet   bakery   hotel   school

4. boots   necklace   shoes   socks

D. Write sentences with *this, that, these,* and *those.*

old

Ex. _____ This car is old. _____

large

1. _____

broken

2. _____

black

3. _____

E. Write these sentences in the plural.

Ex. That house is large.

_____ *Those houses are large.* _____

1. This room is small.

_____

2. That isn't my pencil.

_____

3. Is this your boot?

_____

F. Listen and circle the correct word to complete the sentence.

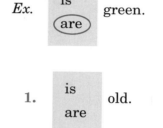

Ex.   is / (are)   green.

1.   is / are   old.

2.   is / are   nice.

3.   is / are   beautiful.

4.   is / are   expensive.

what	language	we	our	is	eat	read
what's	name	you	your	are	live	watch
where	names	they	their	do	sing	speak

A. __What's__ 1 your name?

B. My _____ 2 _____ 3 Sung Hee.

A. Where _____ 4 _____ 5 live?

B. I _____ 6 in Seoul.

A. _____ 7 _____ 8 do you speak?

B. I _____ 9 Korean.

A. What _____ 10 _____ 11 do every day?

B. Every day I _____ 12 Korean food, and

I _____ 13 Korean TV shows.

A. What _____ 14 your names?

B. _____ 15 _____ 16 are Carlos and Maria.

A. Where _____ 17 _____ 18 live?

B. _____ 19 _____ 20 in Madrid.

A. _____ 21 language _____ 22 _____ 23 speak?

B. We _____ 24 Spanish.

A. What _____ 25 you _____ 26 every day?

B. Every day _____ 27 _____ 28 Spanish songs,

and we _____ 29 Spanish newspapers.

A. _____ 30 _____ 31 their names?

B. _____ 32 _____ 33 _____ 34
Yuko and Toshi.

A. _____ 35 _____ 36 they live?

B. _____ 37 _____ 38 in Kyoto.

A. _____ 39 _____ 40 _____ 41
_____ 42 speak?

B. They _____ 43 Japanese.

A. What _____ 44 they _____ 45 every day?

B. Every day _____ 46 _____ 47 Japanese food,
and _____ 48 _____ 49 Japanese TV shows.

B LISTENING

Listen and choose the correct response.

1. (a.) My name is Kenji.
   b. I live in Tokyo.

2. a. They speak Italian.
   b. I speak Italian.

3. a. They watch Russian TV shows.
   b. I watch Russian TV shows.

4. a. We live in Seoul.
   b. They live in Seoul.

5. a. We eat French food.
   b. We speak French.

6. a. They live in Madrid.
   b. We sing Spanish songs.

C PEOPLE AROUND THE WORLD

My name is Jane. I live in Montreal.
Every day I play the piano, and I
listen to Canadian music.

1. What's her name? _____ Her name is Jane. _____

2. Where does she live? _____

3. What does she do every day? _____

(continued)

My name is Omar. I live in Cairo. I speak Arabic. Every day I eat Egyptian food, and I read Egyptian newspapers.

4. _____? His name is Omar.

5. _____? He lives in Cairo.

6. What language does he speak? _____

7. What _____ every day? He _____ Egyptian food, and _____

_____ .

My name is Sonia. I live in Sao Paolo. I speak Portuguese. Every day I do exercises, and I play soccer.

8. What's her name? _____

9. _____ she live? _____

10. What language _____? _____

11. What _____ every day? _____

_____

D WRITE ABOUT YOURSELF

1. What's your name? ....

2. Where do you live? ....

3. What language do you speak? ....

4. What do you do every day? ....

Listen. Then clap and practice.

A. What's his name?

B. His name is Joe.

A. Where does he live?

B. In Mexico.

A. What's her name?

B. Her name is Anne.

A. Where does she live?

B. She lives in Japan.

A. What's her name?

B. Her name is Denise.

A. Where does she live?

B. She lives in Greece.

A. What's his name?

B. His name is Lance.

A. Where does he live?

B. He lives in France.

A. What's her name?

B. Her name is Anastasia.

A. Where does she live?

B. She lives in Malaysia.

A. What's her name?

B. Her name is Maria.

A. Where does she live?

B. She lives in Korea.

EDUARDO'S FAMILY

Fill in the correct form of the verb.

clean	cook	do	live	play	read	shop	speak	work
cleans	cooks	does	lives	plays	reads	shops	speaks	works

My name is Eduardo. I _____live_____ ¹ in Rio de Janeiro. I _____ ² English and

Portuguese. My wife's name is Sonia. She _____ ³ English, Portuguese, and Spanish. Our

children, Fernando and Claudio, also _____ ⁴ English and Portuguese. At school they

_____ ⁵ English and Portuguese books.

We _____ ⁶ in a large apartment. Every day my wife _____ ⁷ the newspaper

and _____ ⁸ in a bank. I _____ ⁹ breakfast and _____ ¹⁰ in an office.

Every weekend we _____ ¹¹ our apartment. I also _____ ¹² at the supermarket.

Fernando _____ ¹³ soccer with his friends, and Claudio and I _____ ¹⁴ basketball.

What languages _____ ¹⁵ YOU speak? What do YOU _____ ¹⁶ every day?

LISTENING

Listen and circle the word you hear.

1. (live)	lives	4. listen	listens	7. sing	sings
2. do	does	5. watch	watches	8. eat	eats
3. do	does	6. eat	eats	9. read	reads

do does	cook	drive	live	paint	sell

1. A. Where _____*does*_____ he live?

   B. He _____*lives*_____ in San Francisco.

2. A. What _____ they do?

   B. They _____ houses.

3. A. What _____ he do?

   B. He _____ a bus.

4. A. Where _____ you live?

   B. I _____ in Sydney.

5. A. What _____ you do?

   B. We _____ in a restaurant.

6. A. What _____ he _____?

   B. He _____ cars.

1. I drive a bus. My friend Carla _____*drives*_____ a taxi.

2. We _____ in a bank. They work in an office.

3. Victor _____ the violin. His children play the piano.

4. I sell cars. My wife _____ computers.

5. I paint houses. My brother _____ pictures.

6. We live in Los Angeles. Our son _____ in London.

J LISTEN AND PRONOUNCE

Listen to each word and then say it.

1. chair	4. Chen	7. church	10. children	13. Sharp	16. Shirley	19. short
2. bench	5. kitchen	8. cheap	11. Richard	14. shirt	17. washing	20. English
3. Charlie	6. Chinese	9. watch	12. shoes	15. machine	18. station	21. French

K LOUD AND CLEAR

Fill in the words. Then read the sentences aloud.

chair	Charlie	kitchen	Chinese

1. ____Charlie____ is sitting in a ____chair____ in his
_____ and eating _____ food.

Shirley	short	shoes

2. _____ isn't _____ in her new
_____.

watch	Richard	cheap	French

3. _____ is looking for a _____
_____ _____.

shirt	washing	washing machine

4. He's _____ his _____ in his
_____ _____.

bench	children	Chen	church

5. Mr. _____ and his _____ are sitting
on a _____ in front of the _____.

Sharp	station	English

6. Mr. _____ is in London at an _____
train _____.

A WHAT'S THE DAY?

1. Monday _____Tuesday_____ Wednesday

2. Friday _____ Sunday

3. Tuesday _____ Thursday

4. Saturday _____ Monday

5. Thursday _____ Saturday

6. Sunday _____ Tuesday

B WHAT ARE THEY SAYING?

Yes, { he / she / it } does. No, { he / she / it } doesn't.

what kind of
when

1. _____Does_____ your husband cook breakfast every day?

   Yes, _____he does_____.

2. _____ your daughter study English in school?

   Yes, _____.

3. _____ your son drive a car?

   No, _____.

4. _____ food does he cook?

   He cooks Italian food.

5. _____ that dog live in this neighborhood?

   No, it _____.

6. _____ your grandfather shop at the grocery store in his neighborhood?

   Yes, _____.

7. _____ your sister work at the bank?

   No, _____.

8. _____ does Robert visit his friends?

   He visits his friends on Sunday.

$$\text{Yes, } \begin{cases} \text{I} \\ \text{we} \\ \text{you} \\ \text{they} \end{cases} \text{do.} \qquad \text{No, } \begin{cases} \text{I} \\ \text{we} \\ \text{you} \\ \text{they} \end{cases} \text{don't.}$$

1. __Do__ you sing in the shower?

Yes, __I do__.

2. _____ your children speak French?

No, _____.

3. _____ you and your husband live in this neighborhood?

Yes, _____.

4. _____ you and your wife play cards?

No, _____.

5. _____ you work on Saturday?

No, _____.

6. _____ your neighbors make a lot of noise?

Yes, _____.

D LISTENING

Listen and choose the correct response.

1. a. Chinese music.
   b. French food.
   c. Every day.

2. a. Yes, he does.
   b. No, we don't.
   c. Yes, they do.

3. a. No, he doesn't.
   b. Because he likes the food.
   c. On Wednesday.

4. a. On Sunday.
   b. Yes, she does.
   c. In her house.

5. a. I go every day.
   b. I don't go there.
   c. Yes, I do.

6. a. In New York.
   b. On Thursday.
   c. They don't go there.

7. a. Because it's open.
   b. They play.
   c. He rides his bicycle.

8. a. No, they don't.
   b. In the city.
   c. Yes, she does.

9. a. Because it's near their house.
   b. On Central Avenue.
   c. Yes, they do.

E   YES AND NO

1. My husband cooks Italian food. He __doesn't__ __cook__ Thai food.

2. Linda drives a taxi. She _____ _____ a bus.

3. Our children play the piano. They _____ _____ the guitar.

4. I work on Saturday. I _____ _____ on Sunday.

5. Tom lives in an apartment. He _____ _____ in a house.

6. My wife and I exercise in the park. We _____ _____ in a health club.

7. Every Saturday Mrs. Roberts _____ to the library. She doesn't go to the mall.

8. I _____ in large supermarkets. I don't shop in small grocery stores.

9. My mother _____ stockings. She doesn't wear socks.

10. Omar _____ Arabic. He doesn't speak Spanish.

11. Harry sings in the shower. He _____ _____ in the jacuzzi.

F   WHAT'S THE WORD?

do	does

1. Where __do__ they live?

2. When _____ your daughter do her homework?

3. What kind of books _____ you read?

4. Why _____ he call you every day?

5. What languages _____ they speak?

6. Where _____ your husband work?

7. _____ you visit your friends every week?

8. _____ he go to Stanley's Restaurant?

9. When _____ you go to the supermarket?

10. _____ your children wash the dishes?

11. What kind of music _____ she listen to?

12. What _____ he sell?

13. Why _____ they cry at weddings?

G   WRITE ABOUT YOURSELF

1. I like ....   I don't like ....

2. I play ....   I don't play ....

3. I speak ....   I don't speak ....

4. I eat ....   I don't eat ....

5. I cook ....   I don't cook ....

1. Does Kathy take karate lessons?

   _____ Yes, she does. _____

2. Do Jim and Tom play tennis on Sunday?

   _____ No, they don't. They play volleyball. _____

3. Do you and Harry go dancing on Friday?

   _____

4. Does Miguel play in the orchestra?

   _____

5. Do you see a movie every weekend?

   _____

6. Do Mr. and Mrs. Kim go to a health club?

   _____

7. Does Richard jog in the park?

   _____

8. Do you and your wife watch TV every day?

   _____

I LISTENING

Listen and choose the correct response.

1. a. Yes, they do.
   b. Yes, I do. *(b circled)*

2. a. Yes, he does.
   b. Yes, I do.

3. a. No, he doesn't.
   b. No, they don't.

4. a. No, she doesn't.
   b. No, I don't.

5. a. Yes, we do.
   b. Yes, he does.

6. a. Yes, we do.
   b. No, they don't.

7. a. No, I don't.
   b. Yes, he does.

8. a. Yes, they do.
   b. Yes, he does.

9. a. No, we don't.
   b. No, they don't.

J **GRAMMARRAP:** *They Do, They Don't*

Listen. Then clap and practice.

Does he	Yes he	No he

A.   Does he eat French   bread?

B.   Yes, he   does.

A.   Does she like Swiss   cheese?

B.   Yes, she   does.

A.   Do they cook Greek   food?

B.   Yes, they   do.

A.   Do they speak   Chinese?

B.   Yes, they   do.

All.   He eats French   bread.

She likes Swiss   cheese.

They cook Greek   food.

And they speak   Chinese.

A.   Does he read the   paper?

B.   No, he   doesn't.

A.   Does she watch   TV?

B.   No, she   doesn't.

A.   Do they go to   movies?

B.   No, they   don't.

A.   Do they drink iced   tea?

B.   No, they   don't.

All.   He doesn't read the paper.

She doesn't watch   TV.

They don't go to   movies.

And they don't drink   tea.

Activity Workbook   **73**

K A LETTER TO A PEN PAL

Read and practice.

Wednesday

Dear Peter,

My family and I live in San Juan. We speak Spanish. My mother is a music teacher. She plays the violin and the piano. My father works in an office.

My brother Ramon and I go to school every day. We study history, English, Spanish, science, and mathematics. My favorite school subject is science. I don't like history, but I like mathematics.

Do you like sports? Every day at school I play soccer. On Saturday I swim. What sports do you play? What kind of music do you like? I like rock music and country music very much, but I don't like jazz. What kind of movies do you like? I like adventure movies and comedies. I think science fiction movies are terrible.

Tell me about your family and your school.

Your friend,
Maria

L YOUR LETTER TO A PEN PAL

history
English
mathematics
science
music

baseball
football
hockey
golf
tennis
soccer

cartoons
dramas
comedies
westerns
adventure movies
science fiction
    movies

classical music
jazz
popular music
rock music
country music

Dear ....,

My family and I live in .... We speak

.... At school, I study ....,

............................., and .... My favorite subject is

.... I don't like ....

What sports do you play? I play .... and

.... I think .... is wonderful. I don't

like ....

What kind of movies do you like? I like .... and

....

My favorite kind of music is ...., and I like

.... I don't listen to ....

Tell me about your school and your city.

Your friend,

....

A. Circle the correct answers.

Ex. We (live) / lives in Tokyo.

1. Tom play / plays in the park.

2. My wife and I shop / shops on Monday.

3. She don't / doesn't work on Saturday.

4. Where do / does your cousins live?

5. We stays / stay home every Sunday.

6. What activities do / does she do?

B. Fill in the blanks.

Ex. ___What___ is your address?

1. _____ does he live?

2. _____ kind of food do you like?

3. _____ Patty baby-sit for her neighbors?

4. _____ do you eat at that restaurant?
   Because we like the food.

5. _____ does Julie go to a health club?
   On Monday.

6. _____ does your family do on Sunday?

C. Fill in the blanks.

Mrs. Davis _____¹ in Dallas. She's a very active person. She _____² exercises every day. On Monday she _____³ her apartment, on Wednesday she _____⁴ tennis, on Friday she _____⁵ a karate lesson, on Saturday she _____⁶ her bicycle in the park, and on Sunday she _____⁷ to a museum and _____⁸ lunch in a restaurant.

D. Listen and choose the correct response.

Ex. a. We go to school.
   b.) They work in an office.
   c. They're shy.

1. a. Yes, we do.
   b. We like dramas.
   c. On Thursday.

2. a. In a restaurant.
   b. Because we like it.
   c. Every day.

3. a. Yes, they do.
   b. Yes, he does.
   c. In Puerto Rico.

4. a. Short stories.
   b. News programs.
   c. I like golf.

5. a. Yes, they do.
   b. Because it's convenient.
   c. On Center Street.

me	us
him	you
her	them
it	

1. Do you like me?
   Of course I like ___you___.

2. Do you like your neighbors?
   Of course I like _____.

3. Do you like Helen?
   Of course I like _____.

4. Do you like George?
   Of course I like _____.

5. Do you like videos?
   Of course I like _____.

6. Do you like English?
   Of course I like _____.

7. Do your friends like you?
   Of course they like _____.

8. Do you like your new apartment?
   Of course I like _____.

9. Does your dog like you?
   Of course he likes _____.

it	her	him	them

1. She washes ___it___ every morning.

2. I think about _____ all the time.

3. We visit _____ every weekend.

4. I talk to _____ every night.

5. He uses _____ every day.

6. We feed _____ every afternoon.

C LISTENING

Listen and put a check (✓) under the correct picture.

1. _____   _____✔

2. _____   _____

3. _____   _____

4. _____   _____

5. _____   _____

6. _____   _____

D WRITE ABOUT YOURSELF

1. I .... every day.

2. I .... every week.

3. I .... every month.

4. I .... every year.

5. I .... every weekend.

6. I .... every Sunday.

7. I .... every morning.

8. I .... all the time.

WRITE IT AND SAY IT

Write the correct form of the word in parentheses and then say the sentence.

1. Carol sometimes (eat) __eats__ Thai food.

2. My neighbor's dog always (bark) _____ in the afternoon.

3. My son never (clean) _____ his bedroom.

4. Ray always (wash) _____ his car on the weekend.

5. My brother sometimes (jog) _____ at night.

6. Amy usually (read) _____ poetry.

7. My mother rarely (shop) _____ at the grocery store around the corner.

8. Dan sometimes (watch) _____ videos on Saturday.

9. Omar usually (speak) _____ English at work.

10. Patty usually (play) _____ tennis in the park on Saturday.

F **MATCHING**

__c__ 1. Walter always washes his car on Sunday.

____ 2. Jonathan never cooks dinner.

____ 3. Carla rarely watches comedies.

____ 4. My grandmother rarely speaks English.

____ 5. Richard usually jogs in the morning.

____ 6. Larry never writes letters.

____ 7. Nancy rarely studies at home.

____ 8. Jane always fixes her computer.

a. She usually watches dramas.

b. He rarely jogs at night.

c. He never washes it during the week.

d. She usually studies in the library.

e. He always eats in a restaurant.

f. He always writes e-mail messages.

g. She usually speaks Spanish.

h. She never calls a repairperson.

G **LISTENING**

Listen and choose the correct answer.

1. a. He usually washes it.
   b. He never washes it.

2. a. My husband sometimes cooks.
   b. My husband never cooks.

3. a. My neighbors are quiet.
   b. My neighbors are noisy.

4. a. They usually speak Spanish.
   b. They usually speak English.

5. a. Jane is shy.
   b. Jane is outgoing.

6. a. I usually study at home.
   b. I usually study in the library.

H WRITE ABOUT YOURSELF

always	usually	sometimes	rarely	never

1. I _____ wear glasses.
2. I _____ eat Italian food.
3. I _____ listen to country music.
4. I _____ go to English class.
5. I _____ watch videos.
6. I _____ read poetry.
7. I _____ fix my car.
8. I _____ visit my grandparents.

9. I _____ watch game shows on TV.
10. I _____ use a cell phone.
11. I _____ clean my apartment.
12. I always _____.
13. I usually _____.
14. I sometimes _____.
15. I rarely _____.
16. I never _____.

I GRAMMARRAP: *I Always Get to Work on Time*

Listen. Then clap and practice.

A.   I always get to   work on time.

    I'm usually here by   eight.

    I sometimes get here   early.

    I never get here   late.

    No, I never get here   late.

B.   He always gets to   work on time.

    He's usually here by   eight.

    He sometimes gets here early.

    He rarely gets here   late.

A.   No! I NEVER get here   late.

B.   Right! He never gets here   late.

J WHAT'S THE WORD?

have	has

1. Do you ___have___ a bicycle?

2. My daughter _____ curly hair.

3. My parents _____ an old car.

4. Does your son _____ blond hair?

5. Our building _____ a satellite dish.

6. Do you _____ large sunglasses?

7. My sister _____ green eyes.

8. We _____ two dogs and a cat.

K WHAT ARE THEY SAYING?

have	has	do	does	don't	doesn't

1. ___Does___ your son ___have___ a bicycle?

   No. He _doesn't_ _have_ a bicycle. He _has_ a motorcycle.

2. Do you have short stories?

   No. We _____ _____ short stories, but we _____ novels.

3. Do your children _____ a good teacher?

   Yes. They _____ a wonderful teacher.

4. What kind of computer _____ you _____?

   I _____ an IBM.

5. _____ they _____ jeans?

   No. They _____ _____ jeans, but they _____ jackets.

6. _____ this store _____ an elevator?

   No. It _____ _____ an elevator, but it _____ an escalator.

80 Activity Workbook

L WHAT'S THE WORD?

1. Tina doesn't have short hair. She has (long) / curly hair.

2. I don't have straight hair. I have thin / curly hair.

3. My brother isn't tall. He's heavy / short .

4. Albert isn't married. He's curly / single .

5. Your baby boy has beautiful blond eyes / hair .

6. His eyes aren't blue. They're brown / straight .

7. We don't live in the city. We live in the house / suburbs .

M TWO BROTHERS

My brother and I are very different. I'm tall, and he's ___short___ ¹. I _____ ² brown

eyes, and he _____ ³ blue eyes. We both _____ ⁴ brown hair, but I have long, straight

hair, and he has _____ ⁵, _____ ⁶ hair. I'm short and heavy. And he's _____ ⁷ and

_____ ⁸. I'm a chef, and _____ ⁹ a doctor. I live in New York. He _____ ¹⁰ in San

Diego. I have a small apartment in the city. He _____ ¹¹ a large house _____ ¹² the

suburbs. I play tennis. He _____ ¹³ golf. I play the guitar. He doesn't _____ ¹⁴ a musical

instrument. On the weekend, I usually _____ ¹⁵ to parties. He doesn't _____ ¹⁶ to parties.

He _____ ¹⁷ TV and _____ ¹⁸ the newspaper.

N LISTENING

Listen and choose the correct response.

1. a. No. I have short hair.
   b. No. I have straight hair. *(b circled)*

2. a. No. I'm single.
   b. No. I'm tall and thin.

3. a. No. He has black eyes.
   b. No. He has brown eyes.

4. a. No. This is my mother.
   b. No. I have a sister.

5. a. Yes. I go to parties.
   b. Yes. I stay home.

6. a. Yes. He's thin.
   b. No. He's thin.

7. a. No. I live in an apartment.
   b. No. I live in the suburbs.

8. a. No. I have long hair.
   b. No. I have curly hair.

O WHAT'S THE WORD?

Circle the correct word.

1. He watches TV [at / with / (in)] the evening.

2. The health club is [in / on / between] Main Street.

3. I'm playing a game [on / to / in] my computer.

4. Ann is sleeping [on / in / across] the yard.

5. He always talks [about / to / with] the weather.

6. I'm looking [from / for / to] a striped shirt.

7. Do you live [in / on / at] the suburbs?

8. Do your children go [to / at / in] school every day?

9. Tim is swimming [with / on / at] the beach.

10. My son is wearing a pair [from / for / of] new jeans.

11. Do you go [in / to / at] work [at / in / on] Saturday?

12. I listen [to / at / on] the radio in the morning.

A WHAT'S THE WORD?

angry	embarrassed	hot	nervous	scared	thirsty
cold	happy	hungry	sad	sick	tired

1. Howard is crying. He's _____sad_____.

2. Helen is yawning. She's _____.

3. Sam is perspiring. He's _____.

4. Frank is shouting. He's _____.

5. Mrs. Allen is going to the hospital.

   She's _____.

6. Peter is looking at his paper and smiling.

   He's _____.

7. Ben's cat is eating. It's _____.

8. Irene is shivering. She's _____.

9. Louise is biting her nails.

   She's _____.

10. Jason is covering his eyes.

    He's _____.

11. Pam is drinking milk.

    She's _____.

12. Bobby is blushing.

    He's _____.

B TELL ME WHY

1. A. Why are they yawning?

    B. _They're yawning because they're_ tired.

    They always _yawn when they're tired_ .

3. A. Why is he shivering?

    B. _____ cold.

    He always _____ .

5. A. Why is she smiling?

    B. _____ happy.

    She always _____ .

7. A. Why are you shouting?

    B. _____ angry.

    We always _____ .

2. A. Why is she crying?

    B. _____ sad.

    She always _____ .

4. A. Why are you perspiring?

    B. _____ hot.

    I always _____ .

6. A. Why are they eating?

    B. _____ hungry.

    They always _____ .

8. A. Why is he covering his eyes?

    B. _____ scared.

    He always _____ .

C GRAMMARRAP: *I Smile When I'm Happy*

Listen. Then clap and practice.

A.   I smile when I'm   happy.

I frown when I'm   sad.

I blush when I'm   embarrassed.

And I shout when I'm   mad.

B.   Are you smiling?

A.   Yes. I'm happy.

B.   Are you frowning?

A.   Yes. I'm sad.

B.   Are you blushing?

A.   I'm embarrassed.

B.   Are you shouting?

A.   Yes. I'm mad.

D GRAMMARRAP: *Why Are You Doing That?*

Listen. Then clap and practice.

A.   What's Fran   doing?

B.   She's working   late.

A.   Working   late?

Why's she doing   that?

B.   It's Monday.

She always works   late on   Monday.

A.   What are you   doing?

B.   We're playing   cards.

A.   Playing   cards?

Why are you doing that?

B.   It's Tuesday.

We always play   cards on   Tuesday.

A. What's Bob doing?

B. He's cooking spaghetti.

A. Cooking spaghetti?

Why's he doing that?

B. It's Wednesday.

He always cooks spaghetti on Wednesday.

A. What's Maria doing?

B. She's dancing.

A. Dancing?

Why's she doing that?

B. It's Thursday.

She always dances on Thursday.

A. What's Gary doing?

B. He's bathing his cat.

A. Bathing his cat?

Why's he doing that?

B. It's Friday.

He always bathes his cat on Friday.

A. What are you doing?

B. I'm _____ing.

A. _____?

Why are you doing that?

B. It's Saturday.

I always _____ on Saturday.

1. A. My sister is cooking dinner today.

    B. That's strange! She never ___cooks___ dinner.

2. A. Our children are studying with a flashlight.

    B. That's strange! They never _____ with a flashlight.

3. A. Victor is walking to work today.

    B. That's strange! He never _____ to work.

4. A. Ann is brushing her teeth in the kitchen.

    B. That's strange! She never _____ her teeth in the kitchen.

5. A. The dog is eating in the dining room today.

    B. That's strange! It never _____ in the dining room.

6. A. Nancy and Bob are dancing in the office.

    B. That's strange! They never _____ in the office.

7. A. Ruth _____ the carpet today.

    B. That's strange! She never sweeps the carpet.

8. A. My parents _____ poetry today.

    B. That's strange! They never read poetry.

9. A. _____ a typewriter today.

    B. That's strange! You never use a typewriter.

10. A. My cousins _____ in the yard.

    B. That's strange! They never sleep in the yard.

F   WHAT'S THE QUESTION?

Choose the correct question word. Then write the question.

| What | When | Where | Why | What kind of | How many |

1. I'm blushing <u>because I'm embarrassed</u>. <u>*Why are you blushing?*</u>

2. They play tennis <u>in the park</u>. _____

3. She reads her e-mail <u>at night</u>. _____

4. I like <u>Brazilian</u> food. _____

5. We have <u>ten</u> cats. _____

6. He's using his <u>cell phone</u>. _____

| What | How often | Where | Why | What kind of | How many |

7. He watches <u>game</u> shows. _____

8. We call our grandchildren <u>every week</u>. _____

9. They <u>play golf</u> every weekend. _____

10. I'm smiling <u>because I'm happy</u>. _____

11. She's eating <u>in the cafeteria</u> today. _____

12. I'm wearing <u>two</u> sweaters. _____

G   WHICH ONE DOESN'T BELONG?

1. her   me   them   (we)
2. noisy   usually   sometimes   rarely
3. does   doesn't   has   don't
4. angry   yoga   nervous   happy
5. Wednesday   Why   What   When
6. smiling   shivering   crying   outgoing
7. clean   sweep   shy   wash
8. year   evening   night   afternoon

As you listen to each story, read the sentences and check *yes* or *no*.

Jennifer and Jason

1. yes ☐   no ☑   Jennifer and Jason are visiting their father.
2. yes ☐   no ☐   Jennifer and Jason are happy.
3. yes ☐   no ☐   Their grandfather isn't taking them to the park.

Our Boss

4. yes ☐   no ☐   Our boss usually smiles at the office.
5. yes ☐   no ☐   He's happy today.
6. yes ☐   no ☐   Everybody is thinking about the weekend.

On Vacation

7. yes ☐   no ☐   I like vacations.
8. yes ☐   no ☐   When the weather is nice, I watch videos.
9. yes ☐   no ☐   I'm swimming at the beach today because it's cold.

Timmy and His Brother

10. yes ☐   no ☐   Timmy is covering his eyes because he's sad.
11. yes ☐   no ☐   Timmy doesn't like science fiction movies.
12. yes ☐   no ☐   Timmy's brother is scared.

I **LOUD AND CLEAR** S! Z!

sorry hospital sick sister Sally	scientist speaking What's experiments

1. _____Sally_____ is _____sorry_____ her

_____sister_____ is _____sick_____ in

the _____hospital_____ .

2. _____ the _____ doing?

He's _____ about his new

_____ .

always	cousin	Athens	busy	is

3. My _____ in _____

_____ _____ very

_____ .

doesn't	Sally's	clothes	husband	closet

4. _____ _____ _____

have any clean _____ in his

_____ .

Steven	it's	sweeping	is	because

5. _____ _____ _____

the floor _____ _____ dirty.

Sunday	Mrs.	newspaper	Garcia	reads

6. _____ _____ _____ the

_____ every _____ .

zoo	students	sometimes	bus	school

7. The _____ in our

_____ _____ go

to the _____ on the _____ .

plays	soccer	friends	Tuesday	son

8. My _____ Sam _____

_____ with his _____

every _____ .

A. Fill in the blanks.

me	him	her	it	us	you	them

Ex. Do you like this book?
Of course I like ____it____.

1. Do you look like your father?
Yes. I look like _____.

2. When my cats are hungry, I always feed
_____.

3. Sally rarely plays with her sister, but she's
playing with _____ today.

4. I say "hello" to my boss every day, and he
says "hello" to _____.

5. We're going to the park. Do you want to go
with _____?

B. Fill in the blanks.

Ex. Betty never talks to her landlord, but
she's ____talking____ to him today.

1. We never feed the birds, but we're
_____ them today.

2. Harriet never _____ to parties, but
she's going to a party today.

3. My children never bake, but they're
_____ today.

4. Tim never _____ his TV, but he's
fixing it today.

5. Amy rarely _____ her kitchen
windows, but she's washing them today.

C. Fill in the blanks.

do	does	is	are

Ex. a. What __do__ you usually do on the
weekend?

b. What __is__ Tina doing today?

1. Why _____ the baby crying?

2. When _____ David and Pam go to the
supermarket?

3. _____ Bob usually dance?

4. Do they work here? Yes, they _____.

5. _____ your parents cooking lunch?

D. Write the question.

Ex. I'm shivering because I'm cold. (Why?)
_____ Why are you shivering? _____

1. They work in a laboratory every day.
(Where?)
_____

2. We get together on Saturday. (When?)
_____

3. He's crying because he's sad. (Why?)
_____

4. She has three children. (How many?)
_____

5. I'm drinking milk. (What?)
_____

E. Listen and choose the correct response.

Ex. a. They're playing soccer.
b. They play tennis.

1. a. They're delivering mail.
b. They deliver mail.

2. a. We're going to the zoo.
b. We go to the park.

3. a. I'm covering my eyes.
b. I cover my eyes.

4. a. No, I don't.
b. No, I'm not.

5. a. I'm studying in the library.
b. I study in the library.

cook	drive	play	skate	speak
dance	paint	sing	ski	use

1. Billy ____can't____ ____ski____.

   He ____can____ ____skate____.

2. Sally _____ _____.

   She _____ _____.

3. Edward _____ _____ pictures.

   He _____ _____ houses.

4. Carla _____ _____ Arabic.

   She _____ _____ Italian.

5. We _____ _____ Greek
   food.

   We _____ _____ Japanese
   food.

6. I _____ _____ a cash
   register.

   I _____ _____ a
   calculator.

7. They _____ _____ tennis.

   They _____ _____ baseball.

8. Harold _____ _____ a taxi.

   He _____ _____ a bus.

B WHAT CAN YOU DO?

Check the things you can do. Then ask other students.

Can you . . .?	You		Student 1		Student 2	
1. cook	❑ yes	❑ no	❑ yes	❑ no	❑ yes	❑ no
2. swim	❑ yes	❑ no	❑ yes	❑ no	❑ yes	❑ no
3. ski	❑ yes	❑ no	❑ yes	❑ no	❑ yes	❑ no
4. skate	❑ yes	❑ no	❑ yes	❑ no	❑ yes	❑ no
5. paint	❑ yes	❑ no	❑ yes	❑ no	❑ yes	❑ no
6. drive	❑ yes	❑ no	❑ yes	❑ no	❑ yes	❑ no
7. play tennis	❑ yes	❑ no	❑ yes	❑ no	❑ yes	❑ no
8. speak Chinese	❑ yes	❑ no	❑ yes	❑ no	❑ yes	❑ no
9. use a cash register	❑ yes	❑ no	❑ yes	❑ no	❑ yes	❑ no

C WHAT'S THE QUESTION?

1. ___Can he cook___ ?
   Yes, he can.

2. _____ ?
   No, she can't.

3. _____ ?
   Yes, they can.

4. _____ ?
   Yes, I can.

5. _____ ?
   No, he can't.

6. _____ ?
   No, we can't.

D LISTENING

Listen and circle the word you hear.

1. (can)	can't	4. can	can't	7. can	can't	10. can	can't
2. can	can't	5. can	can't	8. can	can't	11. can	can't
3. can	can't	6. can	can't	9. can	can't	12. can	can't

actor   actress   baker   chef   dancer   mechanic   secretary   singer   teacher   truck driver

Across

4. She fixes cars every day.
6. He teaches in a school.
7. She acts in the movies.
9. He dances every day.
10. He acts on TV.

Down

1. She drives a truck.
2. He types every day.
3. He cooks in a restaurant.
5. He bakes pies and cakes.
8. She sings on TV.

(Crossword puzzle with answer: 4 across MECHANIC)

F *CAN OR CAN'T?*

1. My brother is a chef in a bakery. He _____can_____ bake pies and cakes.

2. They _____can't_____ sing. They aren't very good singers.

3. _____ Jane drive a truck? Of course she _____.
   She's a truck driver.

4. The chef in that restaurant _____ cook!
   The food is terrible!

5. Of course I _____ fix cars. I'm a mechanic.

6. That actor is terrible! He _____ act!

7. _____ they dance? Of course they _____.
   They're dancers on TV.

8. I'm a very good cashier. I _____ use a cash register.

9. My new secretary isn't very good. He _____ type, and he _____ speak on the telephone.

10. They're very athletic. They _____ skate, they _____ ski, and they _____ play soccer.

11. My friend George can only speak English. He _____ speak Spanish, and he _____ speak French.

G GRAMMARRAP: *Of Course They Can!*

Listen. Then clap and practice.

> She can speak.
> He can speak.
> We can speak.
> They can speak.

A.   Can Anne speak French?

B.   Of course she   can.

        She can speak French very   well.

A. Can the Browns play   tennis?

B.   Of course they   can.

        They can play   tennis very   well.

A.   Can Peter bake   pies?

B.   Of course he   can.

        He can bake   pies very   well.

A.   Can we speak   English?

B.   Of course we   can.

        We can speak   English very well.

have to	do	don't
has to	does	doesn't

1. Can you play baseball with me?

   I'm sorry. I can't. I __have__ __to__ do my homework.

2. Why is Susie upset today?

   She _____ _____ go to the dentist this afternoon.

3. Can your husband fix the sink?

   No, he can't. He _____ _____ call a plumber.

4. Do I really _____ _____ get a haircut?

   Yes, you do. You _____ _____ get a haircut today.

5. _____ Grandma _____ _____ go to the doctor often?

   Yes, she _____. She _____ _____ go to the doctor every month.

6. _____ you _____ _____ work today?

   No, I _____. I'm on vacation.

7. Do you want to go skiing this weekend?

   This weekend? Sorry. We can't. We _____ _____ clean our apartment.

8. Are you bored?

   No. I'm tired. I _____ _____ go to bed.

A BUSY FAMILY

Mr. and Mrs. Lane, their son Danny, and their daughter Julie are very busy this week.

Monday: Dad – speak to the superintendent
            Mom – meet with Danny's teacher
Tuesday: Danny and Julie–go to the doctor
Wednesday: Dad – fix the car

Thursday: Mom – go to the dentist
Friday: Julie – baby-sit
Saturday: Mom and Dad – clean the apartment
          Danny and Julie – plant flowers in the yard

1. What does Mr. Lane have to do on Monday? _____ He has to speak to the superintendent. _____

2. What does Mrs. Lane have to do on Monday? _____

3. What do Danny and Julie have to do on Tuesday? _____

4. What does Mr. Lane have to do on Wednesday? _____

5. What does Mrs. Lane have to do on Thursday? _____

6. What does Julie have to do on Friday? _____

7. What do Mr. and Mrs. Lane have to do on Saturday? _____

8. What do Danny and Julie have to do on Saturday?_____

J **WRITE ABOUT YOURSELF**

What do YOU have to do this week?

....

....

....

....

K **LISTENING**

Listen and circle the words you hear.

1.	has to	(have to)	4.	has to	have to	7.	can	can't
2.	has to	have to	5.	can	can't	8.	has to	have to
3.	can	can't	6.	has to	have to	9.	can	can't

Activity Workbook **97**

can't	baby-sit	go swimming	have dinner
have to	clean the house	go to a movie	study
has to	go bowling	go to a soccer game	wash my clothes
	go dancing	go to the dentist	work

1. I ___can't go swimming___ today.

   I ___have to go the dentist___.

2. Patty _____ on Saturday.

   She _____.

3. Bob and Julie _____ today.

   They _____.

4. Tom _____ today.

   He _____.

5. We _____ on Saturday.

   We _____.

6. I _____ with you today.

   I _____.

M LISTENING

Listen and choose the correct answer.

1. a. She has to go to the dentist.
   b. She can go to the movies.

2. a. He has to wash his car.
   b. He can't go to the party.

3. a. She can have lunch with her friend.
   b. She can have dinner with her friend.

4. a. They have to paint their kitchen.
   b. They can go skiing.

5. a. He has to cook lunch.
   b. He has to go shopping today.

6. a. She has to baby-sit on Friday.
   b. She can't see a play on Saturday.

Listen. Then clap and practice.

A. Where's Joe?

B. He has to go.

A. Where's Ray?

B. He can't stay.

A. Where's Kate?

B. She can't wait.

A. Where's Steve?

B. He has to leave.

A. Where's Murray?

B. He has to hurry.

A. What about you?

B. I have to go, too.

All. Oh, no!

Joe has to go.

Ray can't stay.

Kate can't wait.

Steve has to leave.

Murray has to hurry.

What can I do?

I have to go, too.

O **GRAMMARRAP:** *Can't Talk Now*

Listen. Then clap and practice.

A. I can't talk now.

I have to go to work.

B. I can't stop now.

I have to catch a train.

C. I can't leave now.

I have to make a call.

D. I can't stop now.

I have to catch a plane.

All. She can't stop now.

She has to catch a train.

She can't stop now.

She has to catch a plane.

A WHAT ARE THEY GOING TO DO?

1. What's Larry going to do tomorrow?

   _____He's going to cook._____

2. What's Jane going to do tomorrow?

   _____

3. What are you going to do tomorrow?

   _____

4. What are they going to do tomorrow?

   _____

5. What are you and your friends going
   to do tomorrow?

   _____

6. What's William going to do tomorrow?

   _____

B WHAT ARE THEY SAYING?

1. ____What are____ you

   ____going to do____ tomorrow?

   ____I'm going to____ clean
   my apartment.

3. _____ your mother

   _____ tomorrow?

   _____
   plant flowers.

2. _____ your husband

   _____ tomorrow?

   _____ fix
   the kitchen sink.

4. _____ your cousins

   _____ tomorrow?

   _____
   visit us.

C WHAT ARE THEY GOING TO DO?

are	is	going	go	to

1. We're __*going*__ __*to*__ __*go*__ dancing tonight.

2. They're __*going*__ swimming this afternoon.

3. I'm _____ _____ _____ shopping tomorrow.

4. Brian _____ _____ _____ the library this morning.

5. Rita _____ _____ _____ _____ _____ a party tomorrow night.

6. My friends and I _____ _____ to a baseball game tomorrow afternoon.

7. Mr. and Mrs. Lopez _____ _____ _____ _____ _____ a concert this evening.

8. I'm _____ _____ the supermarket tomorrow morning, and my husband

   _____ _____ _____ _____ _____ the bank.

D GRAMMARRAP: *What Are You Going to Do?*

Listen. Then clap and practice.

going to = gonna

All. What are you going to   do tomorrow   morning?

How about   tomorrow   afternoon?

What are you going to   do tomorrow   evening?

What are you going to   do this   June?

A. I'm going to vacuum all my   rugs tomorrow   morning.

B. I'm going to walk my dog   tomorrow   afternoon.

C. I'm going to visit all my   friends tomorrow   evening.

D. I'm going to dance at my   wedding this   June.

Activity Workbook   101 ⬤

E WHICH WORD DOESN'T BELONG?

1. January   May   (Monday)   April
2. Tuesday   Saturday   Sunday   September
3. autumn   at once   winter   summer
4. Friday   February   March   October
5. him   them   he   her
6. right now   next week   at once   immediately

F WHAT'S NEXT?

1. June   July   <u>August</u>
2. Monday   Tuesday   _____
3. February March   _____

4. summer   fall   _____
5. Friday   Saturday   _____
6. October   November   _____

G MATCH THE SENTENCES

Are you going to . . .

<u>c</u> 1. call your friends on Thursday?

_____ 2. fix our doorbell this week?

_____ 3. visit your aunt next summer?

_____ 4. visit your cousins in April?

_____ 5. fix our windows this month?

_____ 6. call your uncle this June?

a. No. I'm going to visit them in October.

b. No. I'm going to visit her next winter.

c. No. I'm going to call them on Friday.

d. No. I'm going to fix them next month.

e. No. I'm going to call him this July.

f. No. I'm going to fix it next week.

H LISTENING

Listen and circle the words you hear.

1. (this)   next
2. right now   right away
3. Monday   Sunday
4. wash   cut

5. Tuesday   Thursday
6. November   December
7. spring   winter
8. at once   next month

9. autumn   August
10. watch   wash
11. next   this
12. number   plumber

I WHAT'S THE QUESTION?

1. We're going to <u>do our exercises</u> right now.   What _____ <u>*are you going to do right now?*</u> _____

2. She's going to baby-sit <u>this Friday</u>.   When _____

3. We're going to <u>Paris</u> next April.   Where _____

4. I'm going to clean it <u>because it's dirty</u>.   Why _____

5. They're going to <u>go to the beach</u> today.   What _____

6. I'm going to fix the doorbell <u>next week</u>.   When _____

7. She's going to plant flowers <u>in her yard</u>.   Where _____

8. He's going to read his e-mail <u>right now</u>.   When _____

9. I'm going to bed now <u>because I'm tired</u>.   Why _____

J LISTENING

Listen to the following weather forecasts and circle the correct answers.

Today's Weather Forecast

This afternoon:	hot	(cool)	sunny	(cloudy)
This evening:	foggy	clear	rain	warm

This Weekend's Weather Forecast

Tonight:	cool	cold	clear	warm
Saturday:	cloudy	sunny	foggy	hot
Sunday:	foggy	cool	snow	rain

Monday's Weather Forecast

Monday morning:	cold	cool	cloudy	nice
Monday afternoon:	cool	cold	foggy	snow
Tuesday morning:	sunny	cloudy	nice	warm

WHAT DOES EVERYBODY WANT TO DO TOMORROW?

want to	wants to

1. I _____want to_____ have a picnic tomorrow.

2. George _____ work in his garden.

3. Karen _____ take her children to a concert.

4. Mr. and Mrs. Sato _____ go to the beach.

5. You _____ see a movie.

6. I _____ see a play.

7. My friends _____ go to a basketball game.

L **BAD WEATHER**

go skiing	go sailing	snow	be cold
take her son to the zoo	go jogging	rain	be warm

1. What does Richard want to do tomorrow?

_____He wants to go sailing._____

What's the forecast?

_____It's going to rain._____

2. What does Lucy want to do this afternoon?

_____

What's the forecast?

_____

3. What do Carl and Betty want to do today?

_____

What's the forecast?

_____

4. What does Jeff want to do tomorrow morning?

_____

What's the forecast?

_____

M YES AND NO

doesn't want to
don't want to

YES!   *NO!*

1. My parents want to buy a new car.   _____They don't want to buy_____ a motorcycle.

2. David wants to go to a baseball game.   _____ to a concert.

3. I want to wash my car.   _____ my clothes.

4. Nancy and Pam want to play baseball.   _____ soccer.

5. Michael wants to cook Italian food.   _____ American food.

6. We want to study English.   _____ history.

7. Margaret wants to dance with John.   _____ with Jim.

8. I want to work in the garden today.   _____ in the kitchen.

N YES AND NO

I'm	not	
He She It	isn't	going to
We You They	aren't	

1. Steven is going to go swimming.   _____He isn't going to go_____ sailing.

2. I'm going to take a shower.   _____ a bath.

3. We're going to go bowling.   _____ shopping.

4. Barbara is going to go to the beach.   _____ to the mall.

5. My parents are going to clean the attic.   _____ the basement.

6. It's going to be warm.   _____ cool.

7. Robert is going to listen to the news.   _____ the forecast.

8. You're going to buy a used car.   _____ a new car.

Amy is an actress, but she wants to be a baker. She wants to work in a bakery and bake pies and cakes.

1. A. ___What___ ___does___ Amy ___want___ ___to___ be?

   B. _____ _____ _____ _____ a baker.

2. A. _____ _____ she _____ _____ work?

   B. _____ _____ _____ _____ in a bakery.

3. A. _____ _____ _____ _____ _____ bake?

   B. _____ _____ _____ _____ pies and cakes.

Marvin is a baker, but he wants to be an actor. He wants to sing and dance in movies in Hollywood.

4. A. _____ _____ Marvin _____ _____ be?

   B. _____ _____ _____ _____ an actor.

5. A. _____ _____ he _____ _____ work?

   B. _____ _____ _____ _____ in Hollywood.

6. A. _____ _____ _____ _____ _____ do?

   B. _____ _____ _____ sing and dance.

P WRITE ABOUT YOURSELF

What do you want to be? What do you want to do? Where do you want to work?

....

....

....

....

....

....

Listen. Then clap and practice.

> want to = wanna
> wants to = wantsta

He wants to   go.
I want to   stay.
He wants to   work.
I want to   play.

She wants to   eat at a   restaurant.
I want to   eat at   home.
She wants to   eat with   all our   friends.
I want to   eat   alone.

We want to   leave at   seven.
They want to   leave at   eight.
We want to   get there   early.
They want to   get there   late.

Jack wants to   take the   eight o'clock   plane.
Joe wants to   take the   bus.
Bob wants to   take the   six o'clock   train.
Bill wants to   come with   us.

R WHAT TIME IS IT?

Draw the time on the clocks.

1. It's ten o'clock.

2. It's five fifteen.

3. It's nine thirty.

4. It's three forty-five.

5. It's noon.

6. It's half past eleven.

7. It's a quarter to one.

8. It's a quarter after two.

S WHICH TIMES ARE CORRECT?

Circle the correct times.

1. a. It's four o'clock.
    b. It's five o'clock.

2. a. It's eleven thirteen.
    b. It's eleven thirty.

3. a. It's a quarter after nine.
    b. It's three fifteen.

4. a. It's noon.
    b. It's midnight.

5. a. It's half past six.
    b. It's twelve thirty.

6. a. It's two fifteen.
    b. It's a quarter to three.

7. a. It's one thirty.
    b. It's one forty-five.

8. a. It's a quarter to seven.
    b. It's a quarter after seven.

9. a. It's six o'clock.
    b. It's midnight.

T LISTENING

Listen and write the time you hear.

1. ____7:45____
2. _____
3. _____

4. _____
5. _____
6. _____

7. _____
8. _____
9. _____

10. _____
11. _____
12. _____

U ALAN CHANG'S DAY

Alan Chang gets up every day at seven fifteen. He brushes his teeth and takes a shower. At seven forty-five he eats breakfast and reads his e-mail. At eight thirty he leaves the house and drives to work. Alan works at a computer company. He begins work at nine o'clock. Every day he uses business software on the computer and talks to people on the telephone. At twelve o'clock Adam is always hungry and thirsty. He eats lunch in the cafeteria. Alan leaves work at five thirty. He eats dinner at six o'clock and then at half past seven he watches videos on his new DVD player.

1. What time does Alan get up every day? _____ *He gets up at 7:15.* ___

2. What time does he eat breakfast? _____

3. What time does he leave the house? _____

4. What time does he begin work? _____

5. Where does Alan work? _____

6. What does he do at noon? _____

7. What does he do at half past five? _____

8. What time does he eat dinner? _____

9. What does he do at seven thirty? _____

V YOUR DAY

Answer in complete sentences.

1. What time do you usually get up? ....

2. What do you do after you get up? ....

3. When do you usually leave for school or work? ....

4. What time do you usually have lunch? ....

5. When do you get home from school or work? ....

6. What time do you usually have dinner? ....

7. What do you usually do after dinner? ....

8. When do you usually go to bed? ....

GrammarRap: *Time Flies*

Listen. Then clap and practice.

Time flies.
The days go by.
Monday, Tuesday,
Wednesday, Thursday,
Friday, Saturday.
Time flies.
The days go by.

Time flies.
The months go by.
January, February, March, April,
May, June, July, August,
September, October, November, December.
Time flies.
The months go by.

The seasons come,
The seasons go.
Autumn, winter, spring, summer,
Autumn, winter, spring, summer.
Time flies.
The years go by.
Where do they go?
I don't know.

X GrammarSong: *To Be With You*

Listen and fill in the words to the song. Then listen again and sing along.

I'm	going	be	after	day	year	December	April	right
it's	wait	in	past	month	fall	February	July	
you	waiting	to	with	week	summer	September		

Any day, any <u>week</u> ¹, any month, any _____² , I'm _____³

wait right here to be with you.

_____⁴ the spring, in the _____⁵ , in the winter, or the _____⁶ , just call.

I'm _____⁷ here to be with you.

_____ _____⁸ to wait from January, _____⁹ March,

_____¹⁰ , May, June and _____¹¹ , August, _____¹² , October,

and November, and all of _____¹³ . I'm going to wait . . .

_____¹⁴ one o'clock, a quarter _____¹⁵ . It's half _____¹⁶ one, a quarter

_____¹⁷ two. And I'm going _____ _____¹⁸ right here to be with you.

Any _____¹⁹ , any week, any _____²⁰ , any year, I'm going to wait

_____²¹ here to be _____²² you.

Yes, I'm going to wait right here _____ ____²³ with _____²⁴ .

✓ CHECK-UP TEST: Chapters 13–14

A.

Ex. Ted _____wants to go skating_____, but _____he can't_____. He _____has to fix his car_____.

1. We _____, but _____. We _____.

2. Alice _____, but _____. She _____.

3. I _____, but _____. I _____.

B. Fill in the blanks.

is	are	do	does

Ex. When __is__ Harry going to leave the house?

1. When _____ you going to call the mechanic?

2. _____ you have a bad cold?

3. What _____ they going to do this evening?

4. Where _____ you going skiing?

5. What _____ Carol have to do this Tuesday?

6. _____ your son going to take a bath today?

C. *Ex.* Tom wants to move next spring. _____He doesn't want to move_____ this fall.

Dad is going to fix the sink. _____He isn't going to fix_____ the car.

1. I want to teach French. _____ English.

2. We're going to bed at 10:00. _____ at 9:00.

3. Mrs. Miller can bake pies. _____ cakes.

4. Frank has to go to the dentist. _____ the doctor.

5. Jim and Julie can speak Japanese. _____ Spanish.

6. We have to do our homework. _____ our exercises.

D. Every day Helen gets up at 7:30. At 8:00 she eats breakfast, and at 8:30 she goes to work. At noon she has lunch, and at 5:00 she takes the bus home. What's Helen going to do tomorrow?

Tomorrow Helen _____*is going to get up*_____ at 7:30. At 8:00 she's

_____¹ breakfast, and at 8:30 _____² to work. At noon

_____³ lunch, and at 5:00 _____⁴ home.

E. Write the question.

What	When	Where

Ex. I'm going to clean my house <u>this evening</u>.   _____*When are you going to clean your house?*_____

1. She's going to <u>fix her sink</u> tomorrow.   _____

2. He's going to play tennis <u>in the park</u>.   _____

3. I'm going to go to the zoo <u>this weekend</u>.   _____

4. They're going to study <u>Spanish</u> next year.   _____

F. What time is it?

Ex.   It's ten o'clock.

1.   It's five fifteen.

2.   It's nine thirty.

3.   It's noon.

4.   It's two forty-five.

5.   It's a quarter after eleven.

G. Listen to the story. Fill in the correct times.

English _____	Chinese _____	lunch _____
mathematics _____	science _____	music _____

A WHAT'S THE MATTER?

backache	cough	fever	sore throat	toothache
cold	earache	headache	stomachache	

1. He _____has a cold_____

_____.

2. She _____

_____.

3. I _____

_____.

4. She _____

_____.

5. I _____

_____.

6. He _____

_____.

7. She _____

_____.

8. You _____

_____.

9. He _____

_____.

B LISTENING

Listen to the story. Put the number under the correct picture.

_____

___1___

_____

_____

_____

_____

_____

_____

C. GrammarRap: *What's the Matter?*

Listen. Then clap and practice.

A.   What's the matter with   you?

B.   I have a headache.

      What's the matter with   YOU?

A.   I have a cold.

A.   What's the matter with   him?

B.   He has a toothache.

      What's the matter with   HER?

A.   She has a cold.

A.   What's the matter with   Mary?

B.   She has an earache.

      What's the matter with   BILL?

A.   He has a very bad   cold.

A.   What's the matter with   Fred?

B.   He has a backache.

      What's the matter with   ANNE?

A.   She has an awful   cold.

A.   What's the matter with   Jane?

B.   She has a stomachache.

      What's the matter with   PAUL?

A.   He has a terrible   cold.

A.   What's the matter with the   students?

B.   They have sore   throats.

      What's the matter with the   teachers?

A.   They have terrible   colds.

      They have terrible   terrible

      colds!

WHAT DID YOU DO YESTERDAY?

bake	cook	dance	rest	shout	study
clean	cry	paint	shave	smile	type

1. I _____cooked_____ .

2. I _____ .

3. I _____ .

4. I _____ .

5. I _____ .

6. I _____ .

7. I _____ .

8. I _____ .

9. I _____ .

10. I _____ .

11. I _____ .

12. I _____ .

E WHAT'S THE WORD?

| brush | cook | paint | plant | play | study | wait | watch | work |

1. I _____work_____ in an office every day.

2. I _____played_____ the guitar yesterday.

3. I _____ my teeth every day.

4. I _____ flowers yesterday.

5. I _____ dinner every day.

6. I _____ English yesterday.

7. I _____ my fence yesterday.

8. I _____ TV every day.

9. I _____ for the bus yesterday.

F LISTENING

Listen and circle the correct answer.

Ex. I study. yesterday / (every day)   I played cards. (yesterday) / every day

1. yesterday / every day
2. yesterday / every day
3. yesterday / every day

4. yesterday / every day
5. yesterday / every day
6. yesterday / every day

7. yesterday / every day
8. yesterday / every day
9. yesterday / every day

10. yesterday / every day
11. yesterday / every day
12. yesterday / every day

WHAT DID EVERYBODY DO?

bark	clean	cry	drink	eat	ride	sing	sit	skate	write

1. A. What did James do today?

    B. _____He cleaned_____ his apartment
    all day.

2. A. What did your sister do today?

    B. _____ letters
    all morning.

3. A. What did Mr. and Mrs. Porter do
    yesterday?

    B. _____ songs
    all evening.

4. A. What did you and your friends do
    today?

    B. _____ in the
    park all afternoon.

5. A. What did Linda do yesterday?

    B. _____ lemonade
    all morning.

6. A. What did Jimmy do today?

    B. _____ candy
    and cookies all day.

7. A. What did Mrs. Mason's children do
    today?

    B. _____ all afternoon.

8. A. What did the neighbors' dogs do
    yesterday?

    B. _____ all night.

9. A. What did Howard do yesterday?

    B. _____ in the clinic
    all evening.

10. A. What did Grandma do today?

    B. _____
    her bicycle all afternoon.

H PUZZLE

Across

3. ride

4. study

6. eat

Down

1. cry

2. work

4. sit

5. drink

Crossword grid with ³R O D E filled in.

I PETER'S DAY AT HOME

| bake | cook | fix | paint | plant | rest | wash |

1. Thank you, Peter. This is a very good dinner.

3. Look at the car! It's really clean. Thank you.

5. The kitchen looks beautiful. Yellow is my favorite color.

2. This is a wonderful cake, Peter.

4. The new flowers in the garden are beautiful.

6. The sink isn't broken! I can brush my teeth in the bathroom now!

What did Peter do today?

1. _____He cooked dinner._____

2. _____

3. _____

4. _____

5. _____

6. _____

What did Peter do after dinner?

7. _____

J **GRAMMARRAP:** *What Did They Do?*

Listen. Then clap and practice.

washed [t]	cleaned [d]	painted [ɪd]

A.   What did you   do   today?

B.   I washed my   floors.

A. Your floors?   B.   Yes!

B.   I washed my   floors all   day!

A.   What did Mark   do   today?

B. He cleaned his   house.

A.   His house?   B.   Yes!

B. He cleaned his   house all   day!

A.   What did Pam   do   today?

B. She painted her   porch.

A.   Her porch?   B.   Yes!

B. She painted her   porch all   day!

A.   What did they   do   today?

B. They sang some   songs.

A. Some songs?   B.   Yes!

They sang some   songs all   day!

A.   What did you   do   today?

B.   I _____.

A.   _____? B.   Yes!

B.   I _____   all day!

● **120**   **Activity Workbook**

K MY GRANDFATHER'S BIRTHDAY PARTY

At my grandfather's birthday party last night, everybody (listen) ____listened____ 1 to

Mexican music and (dance) _____ 2. My sister Gloria (sing) _____ 3 my

grandfather's favorite songs all evening, and my brother Daniel (play) _____ 4 the

guitar.

Everybody (sit) _____ 5 in the living room with my grandmother and grandfather

and (look) _____ 6 at old photographs. We (laugh) _____ 7, we (smile)

_____ 8, we (cry) _____ 9, and we (talk) _____ 10 about "the good

old days." What did I do at my grandfather's birthday party? I (drink) _____ 11

lemonade and (eat) _____ 12 a lot of food!

L MATCHING

__e__ 1. At the party my brother played _____.

____ 2. Everybody sat and talked about _____.

____ 3. My sister has a sore throat today because _____.

____ 4. We all looked at _____.

____ 5. We listened to _____.

____ 6. I have a toothache today because I _____.

____ 7. I also have a stomachache because I _____.

a. drank lemonade all night

b. Mexican music

c. "the good old days"

d. ate a lot of food

e. the guitar

f. old photographs

g. she sang all evening

1. Jennifer brushed her teeth last night.

   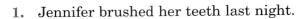
   She didn't brush her teeth.

   She brushed her hair.

2. Kevin played the violin yesterday afternoon.

   _____

   _____

3. Harold and Betty listened to the news yesterday evening.

   _____

   _____

4. Mrs. Martinez waited for the train this afternoon.

   _____

   _____

5. Frank fixed his fence yesterday morning.

   _____

   _____

6. Mr. and Mrs. Park cleaned their attic today.

   _____

   _____

7. Marvin baked a pie yesterday evening.

   _____

   _____

8. Patty called her grandmother last night.

   _____

   _____

ALAN AND HIS SISTER

Alan and his sister Ellen did very different things yesterday. Alan (rest) _____rested_____ ¹ all day. He didn't (work) _____², and he didn't (study) _____³. He (listen) _____⁴ to music yesterday morning. He (watch) _____⁵ game shows on TV yesterday afternoon. And yesterday evening he (talk) _____⁶ to his friends on the telephone and (play) _____⁷ games on his computer.

Ellen didn't (listen) _____⁸ to music. She didn't (watch) _____⁹ game shows on TV, and she didn't (play) _____¹⁰ games on her computer What did she do? She (study) _____¹¹ English yesterday morning. She (clean) _____¹² the yard yesterday afternoon. And she (cook) _____¹³ dinner for her family last night.

C **YES AND NO**

1. Did Alan rest all day yesterday? _____Yes, he did._____

2. Did Ellen rest all day yesterday? _____No, she didn't._____

3. Did Ellen study yesterday morning? _____

4. Did Alan study yesterday morning? _____

5. Did Alan watch TV yesterday afternoon? _____

6. _____Did Ellen clean_____ the yard yesterday afternoon?   Yes, she did.

7. _____ to his friends yesterday evening?   Yes, he did.

8. _____ dinner for his family last night?   No, he didn't.

9. _____ to music yesterday morning?   No, she didn't.

10. _____ game shows yesterday afternoon?   No, she didn't.

11. _____ English yesterday afternoon?   No, he didn't.

D WHAT DID THEY DO?

1. I didn't buy a car. I ____bought____ a motorcycle.

2. Michael didn't have a headache. He _____ a toothache.

3. Alice didn't write to her uncle. She _____ to her cousin.

4. We didn't do our homework last night. We _____ yoga.

5. They didn't take the bus to work today. They _____ the train.

6. Barbara didn't get up at 7:00 this morning. She _____ up at 6:00.

7. My friend and I didn't go swimming yesterday. We _____ bowling.

8. Martha didn't read the newspaper last night. She _____ a book.

9. My children didn't make breakfast this morning. They _____ lunch.

E THEY DIDN'T DO WHAT THEY USUALLY DO

1. Robert usually writes to his friends.
   He ____didn't____ ____write____ to his friends yesterday.
   He ____wrote____ to his grandparents.

2. I usually have a cold in January.
   I _____ _____ a cold last January.
   I _____ a cold last July.

3. We usually eat at home on Friday night.
   We _____ _____ at home last Friday night.
   We _____ at a very nice restaurant.

4. Bill usually gets up 7:00 o'clock.
   He _____ _____ up at 7:00 this morning.
   He _____ up at 10:00.

5. Tom and Tina usually go dancing every week.
   They _____ _____ dancing this week.
   They _____ sailing.

6. Susie usually drinks milk every afternoon.
   She _____ _____ milk this afternoon.
   She _____ lemonade.

7. My brother usually makes lunch on Sunday.
   He _____ _____ lunch last Sunday.
   He _____ dinner.

8. Mr. Lee usually takes his wife to the movies.
   He _____ _____ his wife to the movies last night.
   He _____ his daughter and his son-in-law.

9. We usually buy food at a large supermarket.
   We _____ _____ food at a supermarket today.
   We _____ food at a small grocery store.

10. I usually sit next to Maria in English class.
    I _____ _____ next to Maria yesterday.
    I _____ next to her sister Carmen.

A.   Did she wash her   skirt?

B.   No, she   didn't.

A.   What did she   wash?

B.   She washed her ___shirt___ .

A.   Did they paint the   door?

B.   No, they   didn't.

A.   What did they paint?

B.   They painted the _____ .

A.   Did he call his   mother?

B.   No, he   didn't.

A.   Who did he   call?

B.   He called his _____ .

A.   Did you buy   new suits?

B.   No, we   didn't.

A.   What did you   buy?

B.   We bought new _____ .

A.   Did you get up at   seven?

B.   No, I   didn't.

A.   When did you get   up?

B.   I got up at _____ .

 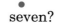

G. WHAT'S THE ANSWER?

1. Did Henry ride his bicycle to work this morning? Yes, _____he did_____ .

2. Did you get up at 6:00 this morning? No, _____ .

3. Did your sister call you last night? Yes, _____ .

4. Did Mr. and Mrs. Chen clean their apartment last weekend? No, _____ .

5. Did you and your friends go to the library yesterday afternoon? Yes, _____ .

6. Did your father make spaghetti for dinner last night? No, _____ .

7. Excuse me. Did I take your gloves? Yes, _____ .

8. Bob, did you do your exercises today? No, _____ .

H. WHAT'S THE QUESTION?

1. _____Did she buy_____ a car? No, she didn't. She bought a truck.

2. _____ a headache? No, he didn't. He had a backache.

3. _____ a shower? No, I didn't. I took a bath.

4. _____ to the supermarket? No, they didn't. They went to the bank.

5. _____ in the living room? No, we didn't. We sat in the kitchen.

6. _____ a right turn? No, you didn't. You made a left turn.

I. LISTENING

Listen and choose the correct response.

1. a. I write to her every day.
   b. I wrote to her this morning.

2. a. He washes it every weekend.
   b. He washed it last weekend.

3. a. They visit my aunt and my uncle.
   b. They visited my aunt and my uncle.

4. a. She did yoga in the park.
   b. She does yoga in the park.

5. a. He went to sleep at 8:00.
   b. He goes to sleep at 8:00.

6. a. We clean it every weekend.
   b. We cleaned it last weekend.

7. a. We take them to the zoo.
   b. We took them to the zoo.

8. a. I make spaghetti.
   b. I made spaghetti.

9. a. She reads it every afternoon.
   b. She read it this afternoon.

10. a. I get up at 7:00.
    b. I got up at 7:00.

I'M SORRY I'M LATE!

forget	go	have to	miss
get up	have	meet	steal

1. I _____missed_____ the train.

2. I _____ a headache.

3. I _____ my lunch.

4. I _____ my girlfriend on the way to work.

5. I _____ late.

6. A thief _____ my bicycle.

7. I _____ go to the bank.

8. I _____ to sleep on the bus.

K **MATCHING**

_d_	1.	buy	a.	wrote
___	2.	steal	b.	did
___	3.	do	c.	went
___	4.	see	d.	bought
___	5.	go	e.	saw
___	6.	write	f.	stole

___	7.	get	g.	had
___	8.	eat	h.	drove
___	9.	have	i.	made
___	10.	forget	j.	got
___	11.	make	k.	forgot
___	12.	drive	l.	ate

L GRAMMARRAP: *Old Friends*

Listen. Then clap and practice.

We walked and   talked

And talked and   walked.

Walked and   talked,

Talked and   walked.

We sat in the   garden

And looked at the   flowers.

We talked and   talked

For hours and   hours.

He drank   milk,

And I drank   tea.

We talked and   talked

From one to   three.

We talked about him.

We talked about us.

Then we walked to the corner

To get the   bus.

We waited and   waited.

The bus was   late.

So we stood and   talked

From four to   eight.

M GRAMMARRAP: *Gossip*

Listen. Then clap and practice.

I told   Jack.

Jack told   Jill.

Jill told   Fred.

Fred told   Bill.

Bill called   Anne.

Anne called   Sue.

Sue told   Jim.

But who told   you?

A TERRIBLE DAY AND A WONDERFUL DAY!

was	were

We ____were____[1] very upset at work last Friday. Our

computers _____[2] broken, our boss _____[3] angry

because he _____[4] tired, and my friends and I

_____[5] sick. Outside it _____[6] cloudy and it

_____[7] very cold. And then in the afternoon all the

trains _____[8] late. I _____[9] hungry when I

got home, and my children _____[10] very noisy. It

_____[11] a terrible day!

We ____were____[12] very happy at work on Monday. Our

computers _____[13] fine, our boss _____[14] happy,

and my friends and I _____[15] energetic. Outside it

_____[16] sunny, it _____[17] warm, and all the trains

_____[18] early. My children _____[19] very quiet

when I got home. We ate a big dinner, and I _____[20] very

full. It was a wonderful day!

B **LISTENING**

Listen and circle the word you hear.

1.	(is) was	4.	is was	7.	are were	10.	is was
2.	is was	5.	is was	8.	are were	11.	are were
3.	are were	6.	are were	9.	is was	12.	are were

C BEFORE AND AFTER

clean	enormous	happy	shiny	thin
comfortable	full	healthy	tall	

1. Before I took A-1 Vitamins, I ___was___ always sick. Now __I'm__ __healthy__ .

2. Before Harold met Gertrude, he _____ sad. Now _____ _____ all the time.

3. Before we ate a big breakfast today, we _____ hungry. Now _____ _____ .

4. Before Helen got her new sofa, she _____ uncomfortable. Now _____ very _____ .

5. Before you drank A-1 Skim Milk, you _____ heavy. Now _____ _____ .

6. Before Charlie used A-1 Car Wax, his car _____ dull. Now _____ _____ .

7. Before these children used A-1 soap, they _____ dirty. Now _____ _____ .

8. When I _____ young, I _____ very short. Now _____ _____ .

9. Before we bought A-1 Bird Food, our birds _____ very tiny. Now _____ _____ .

WHAT'S THE WORD?

1. A. _____Were_____ you at a concert last night?

   B. No, I __wasn't__. I __was__ at a play.

3. A. _____ your boss in the office yesterday?

   B. No, she _____. She _____ on vacation.

5. A. _____ the questions on the examination easy?

   B. No, they _____. They _____ very difficult.

2. A. _____ your neighbors quiet last Saturday night?

   B. No, they _____. They _____ very noisy.

4. A. _____ we at home last Tuesday?

   B. No, we _____. We _____ at the mall.

6. A. _____ Timothy on time for his wedding?

   B. No, he _____. He _____ late.

E LISTENING

Listen and circle the word you hear.

1. was
   (wasn't)

2. were
   weren't

3. were
   weren't

4. was
   wasn't

5. was
   wasn't

6. were
   weren't

7. were
   weren't

8. was
   wasn't

F WHAT'S THE WORD?

did	was	were
didn't	wasn't	weren't

A. Why _____did___¹ Victor leave the party early?

B. He _____² like the party. It _____³ noisy, the food
_____⁴ very good, and his friends _____⁵ there.

A. Where _____⁶ you last week? You _____⁷ at work.

B. That's right. I _____⁸.

A. _____⁹ you sick?

B. Yes, I _____¹⁰. I _____¹¹ very sick. I had an earache and a cold.

A. _____¹² you also have a headache?

B. No. I _____¹³ have a headache, but I had a sore throat.
I _____¹⁴ go to work all week. I _____¹⁵ really sick!

A. How _____¹⁶ your vacation?

B. It _____¹⁷ terrible!

A. That's too bad. _____¹⁸ you like the hotel?

B. No, we _____¹⁹. The bathroom sink _____²⁰ broken,
the hotel room _____²¹ clean, and we _____²² sleep well
at night because the people in the next room _____²³ very loud.

A. _____²⁴ you swim at the beach?

B. No, we _____²⁵. The weather _____²⁶ very cold!

A. _____²⁷ your grandchildren visit you last weekend?

B. No, they _____²⁸.

A. That's too bad. _____²⁹ they busy?

B. My grandson _____³⁰ feel well, and my granddaughter _____³¹
on a business trip. We _____³² sad because we _____³³ see them.

132   Activity Workbook

Listen. Then clap and practice.

A.   Were you late this   morning?

B.   No, I wasn't. I was   early.

A.   Was he sick last   night?

B.   No, he wasn't. He was   fine.

A.   Was her hair very   straight?

B.   No, it wasn't. It was   curly.

A.   Were there eight new   lessons?

B.   No, there weren't. There were   nine.

A.   Was the movie   short?

B.   No, it wasn't. It was   long.

A.   Was the food   expensive?

B.   No, it wasn't. It was   free.

A.   Was I right?

B.   No, you weren't. You were   wrong.

A.   Were the tickets two   dollars?

B.   No, they weren't.   They were three.

WHAT ARE THEY SAYING?

basketball	did	freckles	short	subjects	wasn't	weren't
curly	didn't	hobby	sports	was	were	

A. Tell me, what ___did___ ¹ you look like when you _____ ² young? _____ ³ you tall?

B. No, I _____ ⁴. I _____ ⁵ _____ ⁶.

A. _____ ⁷ you have straight hair?

B. No, I _____ ⁸. I had _____ ⁹ hair.

A. Oh. And _____ ¹⁰ you have dimples?

B. No, I _____ ¹¹, but I had _____ ¹².

A. I'm sure you _____ ¹³ very cute!

What _____ ¹⁴ you do with your friends?

B. We played sports.

A. Oh. What _____ ¹⁵ you play?

B. We played _____ ¹⁶ and tennis.

A. Tell me, _____ ¹⁷ you like school?

B. Yes. I liked school a lot.

A. What _____ ¹⁸ your favorite _____ ¹⁹?

B. English and mathematics.

A. _____ ²⁰ you have a _____ ²¹?

B. Yes, I _____ ²². I played chess.

LISTENING

Listen and choose the correct response.

1. a. I was born last week.
   b. I was born in Japan.

2. a. Yes, I did.
   b. I grew up in Tokyo.

3. a. English.
   b. No, I didn't.

4. a. In Los Angeles.
   b. Last year.

5. a. I was tall and thin.
   b. I didn't look.

6. a. No. I had straight hair.
   b. No. I had dimples.

7. a. I played sports.
   b. I play chess.

8. a. Yes. I'm here.
   b. Yes. My father.

Listen. Then clap and practice.

A.   The teacher was   there,

     But where were the   students?

B.   The students were   there.

All.   Where?

A.   The teacher was   there,

     The students were   there,

     But where were the   books?

B.   The books were   there.

All.   Where?

A.   The teacher was   there,

     The students were   there,

     The books were   there,

     But where was the   chalk?

B.   The chalk was   there.

All.   Where?

A.   The teacher was   there,

     The students were   there,

     The books were   there,

     The chalk was   there,

     But where were the   chairs?

B.   The chairs were   there.

All.   Where?

B.   There.

All.   Where?

B.   Right there!

     Right   there!

✓ CHECK-UP TEST: Chapters 15–17

A. Fill in the blanks.

was	were	wasn't	weren't

1. A. ___Was___ Barbara at work yesterday?

   B. No, she _____. She _____ sick.

2. A. Why _____ you late today?

   B. I _____ late because I _____ on time for the bus.

3. A. Where _____ Grandma and Grandpa last night? They _____ at home.

   B. They _____ at a concert.

B. Complete the sentences.

Ex. Before we washed our car, it ___was___ dirty. Now ___it's___ ___clean___.

1. Before I ate dinner, I _____ hungry. Now _____ _____.

2. When I got my cats, they _____ tiny. Now _____ _____.

3. When we _____ in college, we _____ thin. Now _____ _____.

4. When I was young, I _____ energetic. Now _____ _____.

C. Complete the sentences.

Ex. a. Carla usually studies English. — She ___didn't___ ___study___ English yesterday. — She ___studied___ mathematics.

   b. Paul usually writes to his friends. — He ___didn't___ ___write___ to his friends yesterday. — He ___wrote___ to his cousins.

1. I usually drive to the park on Saturday. — I _____ _____ to the park last Saturday. — I _____ to the mall.

2. We usually arrive late. — We _____ _____ late today. — We _____ on time.

3. My husband and my son usually shave in the morning. — They _____ _____ in the morning today. — They _____ in the afternoon.

4. Bob usually goes jogging in the evening. — He _____ _____ jogging yesterday evening. — He _____ dancing.

5. Margaret usually reads the newspaper in the morning. — She _____ _____ the newspaper yesterday morning. — She _____ a magazine.

D. Write the question.

Ex. _____Did they get up_____ at 8:00?   No, they didn't. They got up at 10:00.

1. _____ his brother?   No, he didn't. He met his sister.

2. _____ her bicycle?   No, she didn't. She rode her motorcycle.

3. _____ a good time?   No, we didn't. We had a terrible time.

4. _____ lunch?   No, they didn't. They made dinner.

5. _____ a movie?   No, I didn't. I saw a play.

E. Read the story and then write about yesterday.

Every morning I get up early. I brush my teeth, and I do my exercises. Then I sit in the kitchen and I eat breakfast. At 8:00 I go to work. I walk to the drug store and I buy a newspaper. Then I take the train to my office. I don't take the bus, and I don't drive my car.

Yesterday I _____got up_____ early. I _____^{1} my teeth, and I _____^{2} my exercises. Then I _____^{3} in the kitchen and I _____^{4} breakfast. At 8:00 I _____^{5} to work. I _____^{6} to the drug store and I _____^{7} a newspaper. Then I _____^{8} the train to my office. I _____ _____^{9} the bus, and I _____ _____^{10} my car.

F. Listen and circle the word you hear.

Ex. (is)
     was

1. is
    was

2. are
    were

3. is
    was

4. are
    were

5. is
    was

6. are
    were

7. is
    was

8. are
    were

Listening Scripts

Page 3 Exercise C

Listen and circle the number you hear.

1. My address is five Main Street.
2. My address is seven Main Street.
3. My address is two Main Street.
4. My address is six Main Street.
5. My address is one Main Street.
6. My address is three Main Street.
7. My address is four Main Street.
8. My address is eight Main Street.
9. My address is ten Main Street.
10. My address is nine Main Street.

Page 4 Exercise E

Listen and write the missing numbers.

1. A. What's your phone number?
   B. My phone number is 389-7932.
2. A. What's your telephone number?
   B. My telephone number is 837-2953.
3. A. What's your apartment number?
   B. My apartment number is 6-B.
4. A. What's your address?
   B. My address is 10 Main Street.
5. A. What's your fax number?
   B. My fax number is 654-7315.
6. A. What's your license number?
   B. My license number is 2613498.

Page 5 Exercise F

Listen and write the missing letters.

1. A. What's your last name?
   B. Carter.
   A. How do you spell that?
   B. C-A-R-T-E-R.
2. A. What's your last name?
   B. Johnson.
   A. How do you spell that?
   B. J-O-H-N-S-O-N.
3. A. What's your first name?
   B. Gerald.
   A. How do you spell that?
   B. G-E-R-A-L-D.
4. A. What's your last name?
   B. Anderson.
   A. How do you spell that?
   B. A-N-D-E-R-S-O-N.
5. A. What's your first name?
   B. Phillip.
   A. How do you spell that?
   B. P-H-I-L-L-I-P.
6. A. What's your last name?
   B. Martinez.
   A. How do you spell that?
   B. M-A-R-T-I-N-E-Z.

Page 6 Exercise B

Listen and put a check under the correct picture.

1. A. Where's the book?
   B. It's on the desk.
2. A. Where's the dictionary?
   B. It's on the chair.
3. A. Where's the ruler?
   B. It's on the desk.
4. A. Where's the map?
   B. It's on the bulletin board.
5. A. Where's the globe?
   B. It's on the bookshelf.

6. A. Where's the computer?
   B. It's on the table.

Page 11 Exercise J

Listen and write the number under the correct picture.

1. Our English teacher is in the hospital.
2. Mr. and Mrs. Sanchez are in the restaurant.
3. Mary is at the dentist.
4. Billy and Jimmy are in the park.
5. Mr. and Mrs. Lee are at the social security office.
6. James is home in bed.

Page 11 Exercise K

Listen and circle the word you hear.

1. Where are you?
2. Ms. Jones is in the bank.
3. We're friends.
4. Hi. How are you?
5. Where's the newspaper?
6. He's from Korea.
7. The computer is on the table.
8. It's in the bathroom.

Page 15 Exercise C

Listen and put a check under the correct picture.

1. He's eating lunch.
2. We're drinking milk.
3. I'm playing the guitar.
4. She's playing the piano.
5. We're cooking breakfast.
6. It's in the classroom.
7. I'm reading.
8. He's watching TV.
9. She's studying mathematics.
10. They're playing baseball in the yard.

Page 20 Exercise D

Listen and write the letter or number you hear.

Ex. A. What's your first name?
   B. Mark.
   A. How do you spell that?
   B. M-A-R-K.
1. A. What's your last name?
   B. Carter.
   A. How do you spell that?
   B. C-A-R-T-E-R.
2. A. What's your telephone number?
   B. My telephone number is 354-9812.
3. A. What's your fax number?
   B. My fax number is 890-7462.
4. A. What's your first name?
   B. Julie.
   A. How do you spell that?
   B. J-U-L-I-E.
5. A. What's your telephone number?
   B. My telephone number is 672-3059.
6. A. What's your license number?
   B. My license number is 5170349.

Page 22 Exercise C

Listen and circle the word you hear.

1. We're cleaning our room.
2. He's doing his homework.
3. She's washing her hair.
4. They're fixing their car.
5. You're fixing your TV.
6. I'm feeding my cat.

Page 24 Exercise G

Listen and circle the word you hear.

1. He's studying.
2. She's doing her homework.
3. I'm feeding my cat.

4. He's cleaning his yard.
5. We're fixing our car.
6. They're washing their clothes.

Page 27 Exercise C

Listen and circle the word you hear.

1. Sally's brother is very tall.
2. Their dog is very heavy.
3. The questions in my English book are very easy.
4. My friend George is single.
5. Mary's cat is very ugly!
6. This book is very cheap.

Page 32 Exercise K

Listen and circle the word you hear.

1. A. How's the weather in Rome today?
   B. It's cool.
2. A. How's the weather in Tokyo today?
   B. It's snowing.
3. A. How's the weather in Seoul today?
   B. It's sunny.
4. A. How's the weather in Shanghai today?
   B. It's hot.
5. A. How's the weather in New York today?
   B. It's raining.
6. A. How's the weather in Miami today?
   B. It's cloudy.

Page 34 Exercise O

Listen to the temperature in Fahrenheit and Celsius. Write the numbers you hear.

1. In Los Angeles, it's 86° Fahrenheit/30° Celsius.
2. In Seoul, it's 32° Fahrenheit/0° Celsius.
3. In San Juan, it's 81° Fahrenheit/27° Celsius.
4. In Hong Kong, it's 72° Fahrenheit/22° Celsius.
5. In Miami, it's 93° Fahrenheit/34° Celsius.
6. In London, it's 56° Fahrenheit/13° Celsius.
7. In Mexico City, it's 66° Fahrenheit/19° Celsius.
8. In Moscow, it's 34° Fahrenheit/1° Celsius.

Page 36 Exercise B

Listen and put a check under the correct picture.

1. In this photograph, my sister is skateboarding in the park.
2. In this photograph, my son is acting in a play.
3. In this photograph, my friends are dancing at my wedding.
4. In this photograph, my uncle is baking a cake.
5. In this photograph, my cousin is playing a game on her computer.
6. In this photograph, my husband is standing in front of our apartment building.
7. In this photograph, my grandparents are having dinner.
8. In this photograph, my aunt is planting flowers.

Page 40 Exercise E

Listen and choose the correct response.

Ex. Is he old?

1. Is it large?
2. Is she poor?
3. Is it sunny?
4. Is he quiet?

Page 43 Exercise C

Listen to the sentences about the buildings on the map. After each sentence, write the name on the correct building.

1. There's a bakery between the barber shop and the bank.
2. There's a school next to the church.
3. There's a department store across from the school and the church.
4. There's a library around the corner from the barber shop.
5. There's a hospital across from the library.
6. There's a police station next to the hospital.
7. There's a hair salon across from the barber shop.
8. There's a supermarket next to the hair salon.
9. There's a video store around the corner from the bank.

10. There's a park between the library and the video store.
11. There's a health club around the corner from the department store.
12. There's a train station across from the health club.

Page 51 Exercise D

Listen and circle the word you hear.

1. umbrellas
2. blouses
3. coats
4. computer
5. shoes
6. exercises
7. dress
8. restaurants
9. necklaces
10. earring
11. belt
12. watches
13. nieces
14. nephew
15. shirts
16. tie

Page 52 Exercise E

Listen and circle the color you hear.

1. My favorite color is blue.
2. My favorite color is green.
3. My favorite color is gray.
4. My favorite color is silver.
5. My favorite color is yellow.
6. My favorite color is orange.

Page 54 Exercise H

Listen and put a check under the correct picture.

1. I'm washing these socks.
2. He's reading this book.
3. I'm looking for these men.
4. They're using these computers.
5. We're vacuuming this rug.
6. She's playing with these dogs.
7. We're painting this garage.
8. They're listening to these radios.

Page 54 Exercise I

Listen and circle the correct word to complete the sentence.

1. This bicycle . . .
2. These exercises . . .
3. These apartment buildings . . .
4. This bracelet . . .
5. These women . . .
6. These sunglasses . . .
7. This car . . .
8. These jeans . . .
9. This refrigerator . . .

Page 61 Exercise F

Listen and circle the correct word to complete the sentence.

Ex. These dresses . . .

1. That house . . .
2. Those people . . .
3. These flowers . . .
4. This blouse . . .

Page 63 Exercise B

Listen and choose the correct response.

1. What's your name?
2. What language do you speak?
3. What do they do every day?
4. Where do you live?
5. What language do you speak?
6. What do you do every day?

Page 66 Exercise G

Listen and circle the word you hear.

1. We live in Paris.
2. Where do you live?
3. What language does he speak?
4. Every day I listen to Greek music.
5. Every day she watches English TV shows.
6. What do they eat every day?
7. Every day I sing Korean songs.
8. Every day she eats Chinese food.
9. Every day he reads Mexican newspapers.

Page 70 Exercise D

Listen and choose the correct response.

1. What kind of food do you like?
2. Do they paint houses?
3. Why does he go to that restaurant?
4. When does Mrs. Miller cook dinner?
5. Do you work in a bank?
6. Where do they live?
7. What do your children do in the park?
8. Does your friend Patty drive a taxi?
9. Why do they shop in that store?

Page 72 Exercise I

Listen and choose the correct response.

1. Do you do a different kind of sport every day?
2. Does Bob write for the school newspaper?
3. Do Mr. and Mrs. Chang live near a bus stop?
4. Does your sister baby-sit every weekend?
5. Does Timmy do a different activity every day?
6. Do your children play in the orchestra?
7. Does your son sing in the choir?
8. Do your parents go to the park every day?
9. Do you play cards with your friends?

Page 75 Exercise D

Listen and choose the correct response.

Ex. What do Patty and Peter do during the week?

1. When do you watch your favorite TV program?
2. Why do you eat Italian food?
3. Does Carlos visit his grandparents in Puerto Rico?
4. What kind of books do you like?
5. Where do your nephews live?

Page 77 Exercise C

Listen and put a check under the correct picture.

1. How often do you read them?
2. I call her every day.
3. I don't like him.
4. I wash it every weekend.
5. He calls us all the time.
6. I say "hello" to them every morning.

Page 78 Exercise G

Listen and choose the correct answer.

1. Henry's car is always very dirty.
2. My husband sometimes makes dinner.
3. My neighbors play loud music at night.
4. My grandparents rarely speak English.
5. Jane always spends a lot of time with her friends.
6. I rarely study in the library.

Page 82 Exercise N

Listen and choose the correct response.

1. Do you have curly hair?
2. Are you married?
3. Does he have brown eyes?
4. Do you have a brother?
5. Do you usually go out on weekends?
6. Is your husband heavy?
7. Do you live in the city?
8. Do you have short hair?

Page 89 Exercise H

As you listen to each story, read the sentences and check yes *or* no.

Jennifer and Jason

Jennifer and Jason are visiting their grandfather in California. They're sad today. Their grandfather usually takes them to the park, but he isn't taking them to the park today.

Our Boss

Our boss usually smiles at the office, but he isn't smiling today. He's upset because the people in our office aren't working very hard today. It's Friday, and everybody is thinking about the weekend.

On Vacation

When my family and I are on vacation, I always have a good time. I usually play tennis, but when it's cold, I play games on my computer and watch videos. Today is a beautiful day, and I'm swimming at the beach.

Timmy and His Brother

Timmy and his brother are watching a science fiction movie. Timmy is covering his eyes because he's scared. He doesn't like science fiction movies. Timmy's brother isn't scared. He likes science fiction movies.

Page 91 Exercise E

Listen and choose the correct response.

Ex. What are Peter and Tom doing today?

1. What do mail carriers do every day?
2. Where are you going today?
3. What do you do when you're scared?
4. Do you usually use a typewriter?
5. Where do you usually study?

Page 93 Exercise D

Listen and circle the word you hear.

1. Our teacher can speak French.
2. I can't play the piano.
3. He can paint houses.
4. My sister can play soccer.
5. They can't sing.
6. Can you drive a bus?
7. I can't read Japanese newspapers.
8. My son Tommy can play the drums.
9. Their children can't swim.
10. Can your husband cook?
11. We can't skate.
12. I can use a cash register.

Page 97 Exercise K

Listen and circle the words you hear.

1. We have to go to the supermarket.
2. My son has to play his violin every day.
3. We can use business software on our computers.
4. Boris has to speak English every day now.
5. I can't cook Italian food.
6. Apartment building superintendents have to repair locks and paint apartments.
7. That actress can't act!
8. Our children have to use a computer to do their homework.
9. Mr. Johnson can operate equipment.

Page 98 Exercise M

Listen and choose the correct answer.

1. I'm sorry. I can't go to the movies with you today. I have to go to the dentist.
2. I can't go to the party on Saturday. I have to wash my clothes.
3. I can't have lunch with you, but I can have dinner.
4. We can't go skiing this weekend. We have to paint our kitchen.
5. I'm very busy today. I have to go shopping, and I have to cook dinner for my family.
6. I can't see a play with you on Friday because I have to baby-sit. But I can see a play with you on Saturday.

Page 102 Exercise H

Listen and circle the words you hear.

1. I'm going to visit her this year.
2. I'm going to write to my uncle right away.
3. I'm going to call them this Monday.
4. When are you going to cut your hair?
5. I'm going to fix it next Tuesday.
6. We're going to see them this December.

7. They're going to visit us this winter.
8. I'm going to clean it at once.
9. We're going to spend time with them this August.
10. I'm going to wash them immediately.
11. You're going to see us next week.
12. When are you going to call the plumber?

Page 103 Exercise J

Listen to the following weather forecasts and circle the correct answers.

Today's Weather Forecast

This is Mike Martinez with today's weather forecast. This afternoon it's going to be cool and cloudy, with temperatures from 50 to 55 degrees Fahrenheit. This evening it's going to be foggy and warm, but it isn't going to rain.

This Weekend's Weather Forecast

This is Barbara Burrows with your weekend weather forecast. Tonight it's going to be clear and warm, with 60 degree temperatures. On Saturday you can swim at the beach. It's going to be sunny and very hot, with temperatures between 90 and 95 degrees Fahrenheit. But take your umbrella with you on Sunday because it's going to be cool and it's going to rain.

Monday's Weather Forecast

This is Al Alberts with Monday's weather forecast. Monday morning it's going to be cool and nice, but Monday afternoon wear your gloves and your boots because it's going to be very cold and it's going to snow! On Tuesday morning the skiing is going to be wonderful because it's going to be sunny and very warm!

Page 108 Exercise T

Listen and write the time you hear.

1. It's seven forty-five.
2. It's six fifteen.
3. It's four thirty.
4. It's nine fifteen.
5. It's midnight.
6. It's five o'clock.
7. It's a quarter to nine.
8. It's a quarter after eight.
9. It's one forty-five.
10. It's noon.
11. It's eleven thirty.
12. It's a quarter to three.

Page 113 Exercise G

Listen to the story. Fill in the correct times.

Every day at school I study English, science, mathematics, music, and Chinese. English class begins at 8:30. I go to science at 10:15 and mathematics at 11:00. We have lunch at 12:15. We go to music at 12:45, and we have Chinese at 1:30.

Page 114 Exercise B

Listen to the story. Put the number under the correct picture.

Everybody in my family is sick today.

My parents are sick.
1. My father has a stomachache.
2. My mother has a backache.

My brother and my sister are sick, too.
3. My sister Alice has an earache.
4. My brother David has a toothache.

My grandparents are also sick.
5. My grandmother has a cold.
6. My grandfather has a sore throat.
7. Even my dog is sick! He has a fever!

Yes, everybody in my family is sick today . . . everybody except me!

How do I feel today?
8. I feel fine!

Page 117 Exercise F

Listen and circle the correct answer.

Example 1: I study.
Example 2: I played cards.

1. I planted flowers.
2. I shave.
3. I cried.
4. I typed.

5. I work.
6. I shouted.
7. I clean.
8. I studied.
9. I fixed my car.
10. I paint.
11. I smile.
12. I cooked.

Page 126 Exercise I

Listen and choose the correct response.

1. When did you write to your girlfriend?
2. When does your neighbor wash his car?
3. Who did your parents visit?
4. Where does Irene do yoga?
5. When did your son go to sleep?
6. When do you clean your apartment?
7. Where did you take your grandchildren?
8. What did you make for dinner?
9. When does Carla read her e-mail?
10. When did you get up today?

Page 129 Exercise B

Listen and circle the word you hear.

1. My husband is thin.
2. She was very hungry.
3. They were tired today.
4. He was very energetic at school today.
5. My wife is at the clinic.
6. Their clothes were clean.
7. My children are very sick today.
8. My parents are home tonight.
9. He was very full this morning.
10. The Lopez family is on vacation.
11. Their neighbors are very noisy.
12. These clothes were dirty.

Page 131 Exercise E

Listen and circle the word you hear.

1. I wasn't busy yesterday.
2. We were at the movies last night.
3. They weren't home today.
4. Tom was on time for his plane.
5. It wasn't cold yesterday.
6. They weren't at the baseball game.
7. My friends were late for the party.
8. The doctor was in her office at noon.

Page 134 Exercise I

Listen and choose the correct response.

1. Where were you born?
2. Where did you grow up?
3. What was your favorite subject in school?
4. When did you move here?
5. What did you look like when you were young?
6. Did you have freckles?
7. What do you do in your spare time?
8. Did you have a favorite hero?

Page 137 Exercise F

Listen and circle the word you hear.

Ex. Is Jane rich or poor?

1. It was a nice day today.
2. My friends were thirsty at lunch.
3. Who is your favorite hero?
4. Were Mr. and Mrs. Parker at home last weekend?
5. My new couch is uncomfortable.
6. My cousins were late for their plane.
7. Before I met Howard, I was very sad.
8. Your children are very cute.

Correlation Key

STUDENT BOOK PAGES	ACTIVITY WORKBOOK PAGES
Chapter 1	
2	2–4 Exercises A–D
4–5	4–5 Exercises E–H
Chapter 2	
8–9	6
10–11	7
12	8–9
14	10–11
16	12
Chapter 3	
18–19	13
20–21	14–17
24	18–19
Check-Up Test	20
Chapter 4	
28	21
29–30	22–25
31	26
Chapter 5	
36–37	27
38–39	28–31
40	32–33
41	34
Chapter 6	
46–48	35–39
Check-Up Test	40
Chapter 7	
56	41
57	42
58	43–44
59–60	45
61–62	46–49
Chapter 8	
68–69	50–51
70	52
71	53
73	54–56
74	57–59
Check-Up Test	60–61
Chapter 9	
80	62–63 Exercises A, B
81	63 Exercise C–66
82	67–68

STUDENT BOOK PAGES	ACTIVITY WORKBOOK PAGES
Chapter 10	
88	69
89	70–71
90–91	72–73
95	74
Check-Up Test	75
Chapter 11	
100	76–77
101	78–79
102	80
103	81–82
Chapter 12	
108–109	83–86
110–111	87–90
Check-Up Test	91
Chapter 13	
118	92–93 Exercise B
119	93 Exercise C–95
122	96–97
123	98–99
Chapter 14	
128	100
129	101
130–131	102–103 Exercise I
133	103 Exercise J–107
134–135	108–111
Check-Up Test	112–113
Chapter 15	
142	114–115
143	116–117
144–145	118–121
Chapter 16	
150	122–123
151	124–125
152	126
153	127–128
Chapter 17	
158	129
159	130
160	131
161	132–133
163	134–135
Check-Up Test	136–137

TEST PREPARATION

A PERSONAL INFORMATION & FORMS

Name: (1) _____

Street: (2) _____ Apartment: (3) _____

City: (4) _____ State: (5) _____ Zip Code: (6) _____

Telephone: (7) _____ E-Mail: (8) _____ Age: (9) _____

Social Security Number: (10) _____ Country of Origin: (11) _____

Look at the information. Choose the correct line on the form.

Example:

062-41-9275
- Ⓐ Line 2
- Ⓑ Line 3
- Ⓒ Line 9
- Ⓓ Line 10   Ⓐ Ⓑ Ⓒ ●

1. Mexico
   - Ⓐ Line 1
   - Ⓑ Line 6
   - Ⓒ Line 8
   - Ⓓ Line 11

2. Los Angeles
   - Ⓐ Line 2
   - Ⓑ Line 3
   - Ⓒ Line 4
   - Ⓓ Line 7

3. 6-A
   - Ⓐ Line 3
   - Ⓑ Line 6
   - Ⓒ Line 9
   - Ⓓ Line 10

4. 90021
   - Ⓐ Line 2
   - Ⓑ Line 6
   - Ⓒ Line 7
   - Ⓓ Line 9

5. 840 Central Avenue
   - Ⓐ Line 1
   - Ⓑ Line 2
   - Ⓒ Line 4
   - Ⓓ Line 8

1 Ⓐ Ⓑ Ⓒ Ⓓ   3 Ⓐ Ⓑ Ⓒ Ⓓ   5 Ⓐ Ⓑ Ⓒ Ⓓ

2 Ⓐ Ⓑ Ⓒ Ⓓ   4 Ⓐ Ⓑ Ⓒ Ⓓ

Go to the next page ➤   **T1** ⬤

B INFORMATION ON AN ENVELOPE

Sally Grant
360 Lake Street, Apt. 4-D
Los Angeles, California 90016

Choose the correct answer.

Example:

last name
- Ⓐ Sally
- Ⓑ Lake
- Ⓒ Grant
- Ⓓ Los Angeles   Ⓐ Ⓑ ● Ⓓ

8. address
- Ⓐ 360 Lake Street
- Ⓑ Sally Grant
- Ⓒ 90016
- Ⓓ California

6. state
- Ⓐ Street
- Ⓑ Grant
- Ⓒ Los Angeles
- Ⓓ California

9. apartment number
- Ⓐ 360
- Ⓑ 4-D
- Ⓒ 90016
- Ⓓ 4

7. first name
- Ⓐ Lake
- Ⓑ Sally
- Ⓒ Grant
- Ⓓ Street

10. city
- Ⓐ California
- Ⓑ Grant
- Ⓒ Lake Street
- Ⓓ Los Angeles

C COMMON ABBREVIATIONS IN ADDRESSES

Look at the abbreviation. Choose the correct answer.

Example:

W.
- Ⓐ East
- Ⓑ West
- Ⓒ North
- Ⓓ South   Ⓐ ● Ⓒ Ⓓ

12. Ave.
- Ⓐ Apartment
- Ⓑ Avenue
- Ⓒ Street
- Ⓓ East

11. N.
- Ⓐ East
- Ⓑ West
- Ⓒ North
- Ⓓ South

13. St.
- Ⓐ South
- Ⓑ West
- Ⓒ Street
- Ⓓ East

. . . .

6 Ⓐ Ⓑ Ⓒ Ⓓ   8 Ⓐ Ⓑ Ⓒ Ⓓ   10 Ⓐ Ⓑ Ⓒ Ⓓ   12 Ⓐ Ⓑ Ⓒ Ⓓ

7 Ⓐ Ⓑ Ⓒ Ⓓ   9 Ⓐ Ⓑ Ⓒ Ⓓ   11 Ⓐ Ⓑ Ⓒ Ⓓ   13 Ⓐ Ⓑ Ⓒ Ⓓ

Go to the next page ⟩

Name _____ Date _____

D GRAMMAR IN CONTEXT: Asking About & Giving Personal Information

Choose the correct answer to complete the conversation.

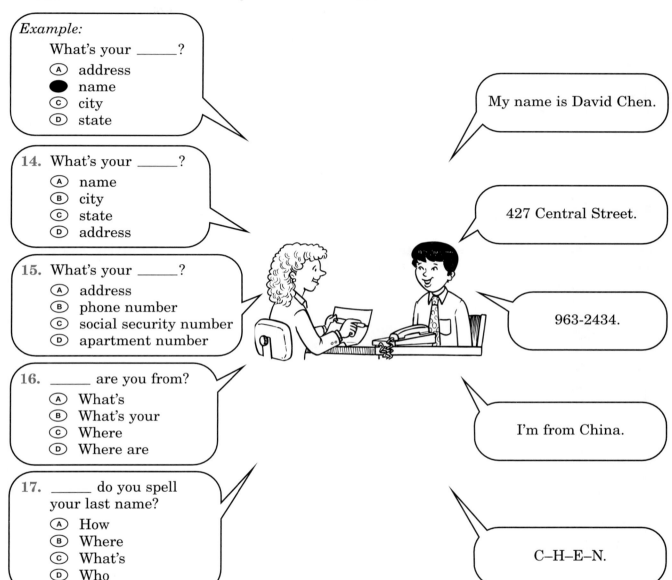

Example:
What's your _____?
Ⓐ address
● name
Ⓒ city
Ⓓ state

My name is David Chen.

14. What's your _____?
Ⓐ name
Ⓑ city
Ⓒ state
Ⓓ address

427 Central Street.

15. What's your _____?
Ⓐ address
Ⓑ phone number
Ⓒ social security number
Ⓓ apartment number

963-2434.

16. _____ are you from?
Ⓐ What's
Ⓑ What's your
Ⓒ Where
Ⓓ Where are

I'm from China.

17. _____ do you spell your last name?
Ⓐ How
Ⓑ Where
Ⓒ What's
Ⓓ Who

C–H–E–N.

E LISTENING ASSESSMENT

Read and listen to the questions. Then listen to the interview, and answer the questions.

18. What's her last name?
Ⓐ Sally
Ⓑ Susan
Ⓒ Keller
Ⓓ Geller

19. What's her phone number?
Ⓐ 68 Central Avenue
Ⓑ 86 Central Avenue
Ⓒ 681-2394
Ⓓ 861-2394

20. What's her address?
Ⓐ 68 Central Avenue
Ⓑ 86 Central Avenue
Ⓒ 681-2394
Ⓓ 861-2394

14 Ⓐ Ⓑ Ⓒ Ⓓ   16 Ⓐ Ⓑ Ⓒ Ⓓ   18 Ⓐ Ⓑ Ⓒ Ⓓ   20 Ⓐ Ⓑ Ⓒ Ⓓ
15 Ⓐ Ⓑ Ⓒ Ⓓ   17 Ⓐ Ⓑ Ⓒ Ⓓ   19 Ⓐ Ⓑ Ⓒ Ⓓ

Go to the next page ⟶ T3

F WRITING ASSESSMENT: Fill Out the Form

Name: _____

Street: _____ Apartment: _____

City: _____ State: _____ Zip Code: _____

Telephone: _____ Social Security Number: _____

Age: _____ Country of Origin: _____

G WRITING ASSESSMENT: Address the Envelope

Address the envelope to Mr. Peter Black. His address is 378 Main Street in Waterville, Florida. His zip code is 33068. Put your return address on the envelope.

_____

_____

_____

                              _____

                              _____

                              _____

H SPEAKING ASSESSMENT

I can ask and answer these questions:

Ask Answer
☐ ☐ What's your name?
☐ ☐ What's your address?
☐ ☐ What's your telephone number?
☐ ☐ What's your social security number?
☐ ☐ What's your age?
☐ ☐ Where are you from?

Ask Answer
☐ ☐ Who is the president of the United States?
☐ ☐ Who is the president or prime minister of your native country?
☐ ☐ Who is the mayor of our city?
☐ ☐ Who is the governor of our state?

T4

STOP

Name _____

Date _____ **Class** _____

A CLASSROOM ITEMS & SIMPLE COMMANDS

Choose the correct answer.

Example:

Open your _____.
- Ⓐ chair
- Ⓑ desk
- Ⓒ book
- ⬤ notebook

1. Go to the _____.
- Ⓐ book
- Ⓑ bookshelf
- Ⓒ board
- Ⓓ globe

2. Give me the _____.
- Ⓐ ruler
- Ⓑ pencil
- Ⓒ clock
- Ⓓ wall

3. Put the _____ on the desk.
- Ⓐ dictionary
- Ⓑ computer
- Ⓒ pen
- Ⓓ ruler

4. Point to the _____.
- Ⓐ table
- Ⓑ map
- Ⓒ globe
- Ⓓ bulletin board

5. Close your _____.
- Ⓐ book
- Ⓑ wall
- Ⓒ table
- Ⓓ pen

1 Ⓐ Ⓑ Ⓒ Ⓓ   3 Ⓐ Ⓑ Ⓒ Ⓓ   5 Ⓐ Ⓑ Ⓒ Ⓓ

2 Ⓐ Ⓑ Ⓒ Ⓓ   4 Ⓐ Ⓑ Ⓒ Ⓓ

B SCHOOL PERSONNEL & LOCATIONS

Choose the correct answer.

Example:

Where's the principal?
- Ⓐ It's in the classroom.
- Ⓑ She's in the classroom.
- Ⓒ He's in the principal's office.
- ● She's in the principal's office.

6. Where are the teachers?
- Ⓐ She's in the hall.
- Ⓑ They're in the hall.
- Ⓒ He's in the classroom.
- Ⓓ They're in the classroom.

7. Where's the clerk?
- Ⓐ They're in the classroom.
- Ⓑ It's on the desk.
- Ⓒ She's in the hall.
- Ⓓ He's in the office.

8. Where's the security officer?
- Ⓐ She's on the wall.
- Ⓑ It's on the wall.
- Ⓒ She's in the hall.
- Ⓓ It's in the hall.

9. Where's the custodian?
- Ⓐ He's in the cafeteria.
- Ⓑ He's in the classroom.
- Ⓒ He's in the hall.
- Ⓓ He's in the office.

10. Where's the librarian?
- Ⓐ She's in the bookshelf.
- Ⓑ She's in the library.
- Ⓒ It's in the school.
- Ⓓ She's in the hospital.

....

6 Ⓐ Ⓑ Ⓒ Ⓓ   8 Ⓐ Ⓑ Ⓒ Ⓓ   10 Ⓐ Ⓑ Ⓒ Ⓓ

7 Ⓐ Ⓑ Ⓒ Ⓓ   9 Ⓐ Ⓑ Ⓒ Ⓓ

Go to the next page ⟩

C GRAMMAR IN CONTEXT: Greeting • Locating Classroom Items

Choose the correct answer to complete the conversation.

Example:
Hi. _____
- Ⓐ Fine.
- Ⓑ Fine, thanks.
- Ⓒ And you?
- ● How are you?

11. _____
- Ⓐ Bye.
- Ⓑ Goodbye.
- Ⓒ Fine. And you?
- Ⓓ How are you?

12. _____ the pencils?
- Ⓐ Where's
- Ⓑ What's
- Ⓒ What are
- Ⓓ Where are

13. _____ on the desk.
- Ⓐ They're
- Ⓑ I'm
- Ⓒ We're
- Ⓓ It's

14. Where's the _____?
- Ⓐ clock
- Ⓑ computer
- Ⓒ dictionary
- Ⓓ ruler

15. The monitor and the _____ are on the table.
- Ⓐ board
- Ⓑ notebook
- Ⓒ keyboard
- Ⓓ bulletin board

16. _____ the floppy disk?
- Ⓐ What's
- Ⓑ Where's
- Ⓒ What are
- Ⓓ Where are

17. It's in the _____.
- Ⓐ dictionary
- Ⓑ keyboard
- Ⓒ disk drive
- Ⓓ desk

11 Ⓐ Ⓑ Ⓒ Ⓓ   13 Ⓐ Ⓑ Ⓒ Ⓓ   15 Ⓐ Ⓑ Ⓒ Ⓓ   17 Ⓐ Ⓑ Ⓒ Ⓓ
12 Ⓐ Ⓑ Ⓒ Ⓓ   14 Ⓐ Ⓑ Ⓒ Ⓓ   16 Ⓐ Ⓑ Ⓒ Ⓓ

Go to the next page ⟹

D LISTENING ASSESSMENT

Read and listen to the questions. Then listen to the conversation, and answer the questions.

18. What's the principal's name?
    - Ⓐ Rosa.
    - Ⓑ Mr. Wilson.
    - Ⓒ Mr. Lane.
    - Ⓓ Mrs. Lane.

19. Where's the teacher?
    - Ⓐ He's in the hospital.
    - Ⓑ He's in the classroom.
    - Ⓒ He's at the dentist.
    - Ⓓ He's the principal.

20. Which student is absent today?
    - Ⓐ Mr. Wilson.
    - Ⓑ Rosa.
    - Ⓒ Mrs. Wilson.
    - Ⓓ Mrs. Lane.

E WRITING ASSESSMENT: Classroom Objects

Write about the objects in your classroom. What are they, and where are they?

....

....

....

F WRITING ASSESSMENT: School Personnel

Write about the people in your school — your teacher, the principal, the security guard, and other people. What are their names? Where are they now?

....

....

....

....

G SPEAKING ASSESSMENT

I can give and respond to these commands:

Give	Respond	
☐	☐	Stand up.
☐	☐	Go to the board.
☐	☐	Write your name.
☐	☐	Erase your name.
☐	☐	Sit down.

Give	Respond	
☐	☐	Raise your hand.
☐	☐	Open the door.
☐	☐	Close the door.
☐	☐	Turn on the lights.
☐	☐	Turn off the lights.

Give	Respond	
☐	☐	Open your book.
☐	☐	Close your book.
☐	☐	Give me a pen/pencil.
☐	☐	Point to the door.
☐	☐	Point to the board.

I can ask and answer these questions about my classroom and my school:

Ask	Answer	
☐	☐	What objects are in our classroom?
☐	☐	Where's the _object_?
☐	☐	What's on your desk?

Ask	Answer	
☐	☐	What's our teacher's name?
☐	☐	What's the principal's name?
☐	☐	Where's the principal?

18 Ⓐ Ⓑ Ⓒ Ⓓ   19 Ⓐ Ⓑ Ⓒ Ⓓ   20 Ⓐ Ⓑ Ⓒ Ⓓ

A COMMON CLASSROOM & HOME ACTIVITIES

Choose the correct answer.

Example:

What's Ms. Jenner doing?
- Ⓐ She's reading.
- Ⓑ He's cooking.
- Ⓒ She's cooking.
- ● She's eating.

1. What's Mr. Gray doing?

- Ⓐ He's studying.
- Ⓑ She's watching TV.
- Ⓒ He's watching TV.
- Ⓓ He's playing cards.

2. What's Miss Lewis doing?

- Ⓐ She's reading.
- Ⓑ I'm reading.
- Ⓒ He's reading.
- Ⓓ It's reading.

3. What are your friends doing?

- Ⓐ He's playing the guitar.
- Ⓑ They're playing the guitar.
- Ⓒ She's playing baseball.
- Ⓓ They're playing baseball.

4. What's your dog doing?

- Ⓐ I'm sleeping.
- Ⓑ It's sleeping.
- Ⓒ We're sleeping.
- Ⓓ They're sleeping.

5. What are you and Carla doing?

- Ⓐ I'm studying English.
- Ⓑ They're studying English.
- Ⓒ We're studying English.
- Ⓓ She's studying English.

6. What's Mrs. Carter doing?

- Ⓐ He's teaching.
- Ⓑ She's teaching.
- Ⓒ He's playing.
- Ⓓ She's planting.

7. What's Jimmy doing?

- Ⓐ He's playing the piano.
- Ⓑ He's playing baseball.
- Ⓒ He's playing with the dog.
- Ⓓ He's playing the guitar.

8. What are Mr. and Mrs. Lu doing?

- Ⓐ We're eating.
- Ⓑ They're eating.
- Ⓒ They're cooking.
- Ⓓ We're cooking.

9. What are the students doing?

- Ⓐ They're studying English.
- Ⓑ We're studying English.
- Ⓒ I'm studying mathematics.
- Ⓓ He's studying mathematics.

10. What am I doing?

- Ⓐ She's reading a book.
- Ⓑ He's reading the newspaper.
- Ⓒ You're reading a book.
- Ⓓ I'm reading the newspaper.

11. What are your friends doing?

- Ⓐ We're singing.
- Ⓑ You're singing.
- Ⓒ I'm singing.
- Ⓓ They're singing.

1 Ⓐ Ⓑ Ⓒ Ⓓ   4 Ⓐ Ⓑ Ⓒ Ⓓ   7 Ⓐ Ⓑ Ⓒ Ⓓ   10 Ⓐ Ⓑ Ⓒ Ⓓ

2 Ⓐ Ⓑ Ⓒ Ⓓ   5 Ⓐ Ⓑ Ⓒ Ⓓ   8 Ⓐ Ⓑ Ⓒ Ⓓ   11 Ⓐ Ⓑ Ⓒ Ⓓ

3 Ⓐ Ⓑ Ⓒ Ⓓ   6 Ⓐ Ⓑ Ⓒ Ⓓ   9 Ⓐ Ⓑ Ⓒ Ⓓ

Go to the next page   **T9**

B GRAMMAR IN CONTEXT: Asking About Home Activities • Checking Understanding

Choose the correct answer to complete the conversation.

12. Where are _____?
  - Ⓐ I
  - Ⓑ she
  - Ⓒ he
  - Ⓓ you

13. _____ in the kitchen.
  - Ⓐ I'm
  - Ⓑ She's
  - Ⓒ They're
  - Ⓓ It's

14. In the _____?
  - Ⓐ hospital
  - Ⓑ park
  - Ⓒ kitchen
  - Ⓓ classroom

15. Yes. I'm _____.
  - Ⓐ kitchen
  - Ⓑ in the kitchen
  - Ⓒ the kitchen
  - Ⓓ doing

16. What _____ you doing?
  - Ⓐ am
  - Ⓑ are
  - Ⓒ is
  - Ⓓ I

17. _____ cooking.
  - Ⓐ You're
  - Ⓑ They're
  - Ⓒ I'm
  - Ⓓ She's

C LISTENING ASSESSMENT

Read and listen to the questions. Then listen to the story, and answer the questions.

18. What are Mr. and Mrs. Baker doing?
  - Ⓐ They're eating.
  - Ⓑ They're swimming.
  - Ⓒ He's reading.
  - Ⓓ They're reading.

19. What's Tommy doing?
  - Ⓐ He's swimming.
  - Ⓑ He's reading.
  - Ⓒ He's listening to music.
  - Ⓓ She's listening to music.

20. Where are they today?
  - Ⓐ It's a beautiful day.
  - Ⓑ They're very happy.
  - Ⓒ They're at home.
  - Ⓓ They're at the beach.

D WRITING ASSESSMENT

What are you doing now? What are your friends doing?

....

....

E SPEAKING ASSESSMENT

I can ask and answer these questions:

Ask Answer
- ☐ ☐ Where are you?
- ☐ ☐ What are you doing?

Ask Answer
- ☐ ☐ What are other students doing?
- ☐ ☐ What are your friends doing?

12 Ⓐ Ⓑ Ⓒ Ⓓ   15 Ⓐ Ⓑ Ⓒ Ⓓ   18 Ⓐ Ⓑ Ⓒ Ⓓ

13 Ⓐ Ⓑ Ⓒ Ⓓ   16 Ⓐ Ⓑ Ⓒ Ⓓ   19 Ⓐ Ⓑ Ⓒ Ⓓ

14 Ⓐ Ⓑ Ⓒ Ⓓ   17 Ⓐ Ⓑ Ⓒ Ⓓ   20 Ⓐ Ⓑ Ⓒ Ⓓ

STOP

A COMMON CLASSROOM & HOME ACTIVITIES

Choose the best answer.

Example:

He's brushing _____ teeth.
- Ⓐ my
- Ⓑ our
- Ⓒ his
- Ⓓ your   Ⓐ Ⓑ ● Ⓓ

1. She's doing _____ homework.
   - Ⓐ my
   - Ⓑ its
   - Ⓒ our
   - Ⓓ her

2. They're opening _____ books.
   - Ⓐ my
   - Ⓑ their
   - Ⓒ her
   - Ⓓ his

3. I'm brushing _____ teeth.
   - Ⓐ their
   - Ⓑ my
   - Ⓒ its
   - Ⓓ his

4. He's raising _____ hand.
   - Ⓐ our
   - Ⓑ her
   - Ⓒ his
   - Ⓓ their

5. We're doing _____ exercises.
   - Ⓐ our
   - Ⓑ their
   - Ⓒ his
   - Ⓓ her

6. What's Mr. Sharp doing?
   - Ⓐ She's cleaning her kitchen.
   - Ⓑ We're cleaning our kitchen.
   - Ⓒ He's cleaning his kitchen.
   - Ⓓ I'm cleaning my kitchen.

7. What are Mr. and Mrs. Lee doing?
   - Ⓐ He's washing his car.
   - Ⓑ She's washing her car.
   - Ⓒ We're washing our car.
   - Ⓓ They're washing their car.

8. Is Ms. Harris busy?
   - Ⓐ Yes, he is.
   - Ⓑ Yes, I am.
   - Ⓒ Yes, she is.
   - Ⓓ Yes, it is.

9. Are you busy?
   - Ⓐ Yes, you are.
   - Ⓑ Yes, I am.
   - Ⓒ Yes, they are.
   - Ⓓ Yes, it is.

10. Are the students studying?
    - Ⓐ Yes, they are.
    - Ⓑ Yes, you are.
    - Ⓒ Yes, I am.
    - Ⓓ Yes, he is.

11. What are your friends doing?
    - Ⓐ We're painting our apartment.
    - Ⓑ She's painting her apartment.
    - Ⓒ I'm painting my apartment.
    - Ⓓ They're painting their apartment.

1 Ⓐ Ⓑ Ⓒ Ⓓ   4 Ⓐ Ⓑ Ⓒ Ⓓ   7 Ⓐ Ⓑ Ⓒ Ⓓ   10 Ⓐ Ⓑ Ⓒ Ⓓ

2 Ⓐ Ⓑ Ⓒ Ⓓ   5 Ⓐ Ⓑ Ⓒ Ⓓ   8 Ⓐ Ⓑ Ⓒ Ⓓ   11 Ⓐ Ⓑ Ⓒ Ⓓ

3 Ⓐ Ⓑ Ⓒ Ⓓ   6 Ⓐ Ⓑ Ⓒ Ⓓ   9 Ⓐ Ⓑ Ⓒ Ⓓ

Go to the next page > **T11**

B GRAMMAR IN CONTEXT: Getting Someone's Attention • Asking About Home Activities

Choose the correct answer to complete the conversation.

12. Excuse me. Alex?
    _____ you busy?
    - (A) Am
    - (B) Is
    - (C) Are
    - (D) I

13. Yes, _____.
    - (A) we are
    - (B) they are
    - (C) he is
    - (D) I am

14. What _____ doing?
    - (A) are they
    - (B) are you
    - (C) am I
    - (D) is she

15. I'm _____.
    - (A) doing their homework
    - (B) doing its exercises
    - (C) doing my homework
    - (D) doing their exercises

16. _____ Bob doing?
    - (A) What
    - (B) What are
    - (C) Where's
    - (D) What's

17. _____ washing _____ car.
    - (A) He's . . his
    - (B) They're . . their
    - (C) We're . . our
    - (D) I'm . . my

C LISTENING ASSESSMENT

Read and listen to the questions. Then listen to the telephone conversation, and answer the questions.

18. What's Lisa doing?
    - (A) She's washing her car.
    - (B) She's washing her cat.
    - (C) She's watching her windows.
    - (D) She's washing her windows.

19. What's Richard doing?
    - (A) He's doing his homework.
    - (B) He's cooking breakfast.
    - (C) He's cooking dinner.
    - (D) He's cooking lunch.

20. What are the children doing?
    - (A) They're cooking.
    - (B) They're doing their exercises.
    - (C) They're cleaning.
    - (D) They're doing their homework.

D LEARNING SKILL ASSESSMENT: Alphabetizing

Alphabetize the list of names. Write the names in alphabetical (ABC) order.

Molina _____ *Chang* _____

Chang _____

Williams _____

Lopez _____

Gomez _____

E WRITING ASSESSMENT

Write a paragraph about the picture on page 31 of *Side by Side* Book 1. What are the people doing? (Use a separate sheet of paper.)

F SPEAKING ASSESSMENT

I can ask and answer these questions:

Ask Answer
- ☐ ☐ Are you busy?
- ☐ ☐ What are you doing now?
- ☐ ☐ What are your neighbors doing?

12 (A) (B) (C) (D)   15 (A) (B) (C) (D)   18 (A) (B) (C) (D)

13 (A) (B) (C) (D)   16 (A) (B) (C) (D)   19 (A) (B) (C) (D)

14 (A) (B) (C) (D)   17 (A) (B) (C) (D)   20 (A) (B) (C) (D)

STOP

Name _____

Date _____ Class _____

A DESCRIBING PEOPLE, THINGS, & WEATHER

Choose the best answer.

Example:

Is his car new or _____?
- Ⓐ small
- Ⓑ easy
- Ⓒ old
- Ⓓ thin   Ⓐ Ⓑ ● Ⓓ

1. Is her dog big or _____?
- Ⓐ new
- Ⓑ difficult
- Ⓒ noisy
- Ⓓ little

2. Is your brother single or _____?
- Ⓐ tall
- Ⓑ married
- Ⓒ young
- Ⓓ old

3. Are your neighbors quiet or _____?
- Ⓐ noisy
- Ⓑ cheap
- Ⓒ large
- Ⓓ expensive

4. Is your computer old or _____?
- Ⓐ small
- Ⓑ young
- Ⓒ new
- Ⓓ pretty

5. Is it sunny or _____?
- Ⓐ cold
- Ⓑ cloudy
- Ⓒ cool
- Ⓓ hot

6. _____ is pretty.
- Ⓐ Jill cat
- Ⓑ Cat Jill
- Ⓒ Jill's cat
- Ⓓ Jill's cats

7. _____ is large.
- Ⓐ Mr. Grant's car's
- Ⓑ Mr. Grant's cars
- Ⓒ Mr. Grant car
- Ⓓ Mr. Grant's car

8. The questions in our book _____.
- Ⓐ is difficult
- Ⓑ are difficult
- Ⓒ am difficult
- Ⓓ not difficult

9. Is it raining?
- Ⓐ Yes, he is.
- Ⓑ Yes, I am.
- Ⓒ No, it isn't.
- Ⓓ No, we aren't.

10. Are you married?
- Ⓐ No, you aren't.
- Ⓑ No, they aren't.
- Ⓒ No, he isn't.
- Ⓓ No, I'm not.

11. How's the weather?
- Ⓐ It's cool.
- Ⓑ It's cheap.
- Ⓒ It's short.
- Ⓓ It's thin.

....

1 Ⓐ Ⓑ Ⓒ Ⓓ   4 Ⓐ Ⓑ Ⓒ Ⓓ   7 Ⓐ Ⓑ Ⓒ Ⓓ   10 Ⓐ Ⓑ Ⓒ Ⓓ

2 Ⓐ Ⓑ Ⓒ Ⓓ   5 Ⓐ Ⓑ Ⓒ Ⓓ   8 Ⓐ Ⓑ Ⓒ Ⓓ   11 Ⓐ Ⓑ Ⓒ Ⓓ

3 Ⓐ Ⓑ Ⓒ Ⓓ   6 Ⓐ Ⓑ Ⓒ Ⓓ   9 Ⓐ Ⓑ Ⓒ Ⓓ

B GRAMMAR IN CONTEXT: Using the Telephone • Weather

Choose the correct answer to complete the conversation.

Example:

_____
- Ⓐ Yes, it is.
- Ⓑ I'm calling.
- ● Hello.
- Ⓓ Goodbye.

12. Hi, Ann. _____
I'm calling from Honolulu.
- Ⓐ Hello.
- Ⓑ Is this Jim?
- Ⓒ Am I Jim?
- Ⓓ This is Jim.

13. _____
How's the weather in Honolulu?
- Ⓐ Hello. This is Ann.
- Ⓑ Hello. Is this Jim?
- Ⓒ Hi, Jim.
- Ⓓ Yes, it is.

14. The weather is beautiful. It's hot and _____.
- Ⓐ snowing
- Ⓑ sunny
- Ⓒ cold
- Ⓓ cool

C INTERPRETING A THERMOMETER

°F	°C	
100	38	Ⓐ
70	21	Ⓑ
50	10	Ⓒ
32	0	Ⓓ

For each weather expression, choose the correct temperature on the thermometer.

Example:
It's warm. Ⓐ ● Ⓒ Ⓓ

15. It's cold.

16. It's hot.

17. It's cool.

D LISTENING ASSESSMENT: Weather Report

Read and listen to the questions. Then listen to the weather report, and answer the questions.

18. How's the weather in Miami?
- Ⓐ It's cool.
- Ⓑ It's raining.
- Ⓒ It's snowing.
- Ⓓ It's sunny.

19. What's the temperature in Los Angeles?
- Ⓐ 40°F.
- Ⓑ 95°F.
- Ⓒ 80°F.
- Ⓓ It's hot.

20. How's the weather in New York?
- Ⓐ It's hot.
- Ⓑ It's cold.
- Ⓒ It's snowing.
- Ⓓ It's warm.

E WRITING ASSESSMENT: Form

Name: _____

Social Security Number: _____

Marital Status: _____

F SPEAKING ASSESSMENT

I can ask and answer these questions:

Ask Answer
- ☐ ☐ What's your marital status?
- ☐ ☐ Are you married or single?
- ☐ ☐ How's the weather today?

12 Ⓐ Ⓑ Ⓒ Ⓓ   15 Ⓐ Ⓑ Ⓒ Ⓓ   18 Ⓐ Ⓑ Ⓒ Ⓓ

13 Ⓐ Ⓑ Ⓒ Ⓓ   16 Ⓐ Ⓑ Ⓒ Ⓓ   19 Ⓐ Ⓑ Ⓒ Ⓓ

14 Ⓐ Ⓑ Ⓒ Ⓓ   17 Ⓐ Ⓑ Ⓒ Ⓓ   20 Ⓐ Ⓑ Ⓒ Ⓓ

STOP

A FAMILY RELATIONS

Look at the picture. Choose the correct answer.

John   Kate

Billy   Ann

Example:

John is Kate's _____.

- Ⓐ wife
- Ⓑ husband
- Ⓒ daughter
- Ⓓ son   Ⓐ ● Ⓒ Ⓓ

1. Billy is John and Kate's _____.
   - Ⓐ brother
   - Ⓑ father
   - Ⓒ uncle
   - Ⓓ son

2. Ann is Billy's _____.
   - Ⓐ daughter
   - Ⓑ cousin
   - Ⓒ sister
   - Ⓓ mother

3. John and Kate are Billy and Ann's _____.
   - Ⓐ children
   - Ⓑ parents
   - Ⓒ grandparents
   - Ⓓ aunt and uncle

Look at the picture. Choose the correct answer.

Henry   Peggy

Kate

Billy   Ann

4. Henry is Billy and Ann's _____.
   - Ⓐ grandson
   - Ⓑ granddaughter
   - Ⓒ grandfather
   - Ⓓ grandmother

5. Ann is Peggy and Henry's _____.
   - Ⓐ granddaughter
   - Ⓑ daughter
   - Ⓒ mother
   - Ⓓ sister

6. Henry and Peggy are Billy and Ann's _____.
   - Ⓐ children
   - Ⓑ parents
   - Ⓒ grandparents
   - Ⓓ grandchildren

7. Ann and Billy are Henry and Peggy's _____.
   - Ⓐ children
   - Ⓑ grandparents
   - Ⓒ parents
   - Ⓓ grandchildren

1 Ⓐ Ⓑ Ⓒ Ⓓ   3 Ⓐ Ⓑ Ⓒ Ⓓ   5 Ⓐ Ⓑ Ⓒ Ⓓ   7 Ⓐ Ⓑ Ⓒ Ⓓ

2 Ⓐ Ⓑ Ⓒ Ⓓ   4 Ⓐ Ⓑ Ⓒ Ⓓ   6 Ⓐ Ⓑ Ⓒ Ⓓ

B FAMILY RELATIONS & COMMON ACTIVITIES

Choose the correct answer.

Example:

My _____ is feeding his cat.
- (A) daughter
- (B) wife
- (C) uncle
- (D) mother

(A) (B) ● (D)

11. My _____ is painting her living room.
- (A) aunt
- (B) uncle
- (C) father
- (D) brother

8. My _____ is doing her homework.
- (A) brother
- (B) son
- (C) nephew
- (D) niece

12. My _____ are doing their exercises.
- (A) sisters
- (B) parents
- (C) aunts
- (D) nieces

9. My _____ is washing his hair.
- (A) niece
- (B) nephew
- (C) aunt
- (D) cousins

13. _____ her windows.
- (A) My brother is watching
- (B) My sister is watching
- (C) My brother is washing
- (D) My sister is washing

10. My _____ are brushing their teeth.
- (A) aunt
- (B) uncle
- (C) cousins
- (D) sister

14. _____ TV.
- (A) My parents are washing
- (B) My uncles are washing
- (C) My aunt and uncle are watching
- (D) My aunts are watching

- -

8 (A) (B) (C) (D)   10 (A) (B) (C) (D)   12 (A) (B) (C) (D)   14 (A) (B) (C) (D)

9 (A) (B) (C) (D)   11 (A) (B) (C) (D)   13 (A) (B) (C) (D)

Go to the next page ⟩

C GRAMMAR IN CONTEXT: Greeting & Introducing

Choose the correct answer to complete the conversation.

Example:

Hello. _____
- Ⓐ Is this Brenda?
- Ⓑ How are you?
- Ⓒ Who are you?
- Ⓓ How's the weather?

16. Fine, thanks.
_____ my sister.
- Ⓐ I'm
- Ⓑ Nice to meet
- Ⓒ Her name is
- Ⓓ I'd like to introduce

15. Fine. _____
- Ⓐ Where are you?
- Ⓑ What are you doing?
- Ⓒ And you?
- Ⓓ Yes, I am.

17. _____
- Ⓐ Fine, thanks.
- Ⓑ And you?
- Ⓒ Nice to meet you.
- Ⓓ Nice to meet you, too.

D LISTENING ASSESSMENT

Read and listen to the questions. Then listen to the story, and answer the questions.

18. What day is it?
- Ⓐ It's a beautiful day.
- Ⓑ He's happy.
- Ⓒ It's his wedding day.
- Ⓓ It's his birthday.

19. What are his parents doing?
- Ⓐ They're eating cake.
- Ⓑ They're sitting in the living room.
- Ⓒ They're dancing.
- Ⓓ They're taking photographs.

20. What's his grandfather doing?
- Ⓐ He's dancing.
- Ⓑ He's taking photographs.
- Ⓒ He's eating cake.
- Ⓓ He's old.

E LEARNING SKILL: Categorizing

Write each word in the correct column.

| aunt | daughter | husband | sister | uncle |
| brother | father | mother | son | wife |

Male   **Female**

____brother____   ____aunt____

_____   _____

_____   _____

_____   _____

_____   _____

F EYE CONTACT & GESTURES

For each sentence, choose the correct picture.

A

B

C

D

1. "Patty, this is Mr. Fisher." _____

2. "I'd like to introduce my sister." _____

3. "May I ask a question?" _____

4. "Hello. My name is Peter." _____

G WRITING ASSESSMENT

Write about the people in your family—sisters, brothers, parents, children, grandparents.
What are their names? (Use a separate sheet of paper.)

H SPEAKING ASSESSMENT

I can introduce myself and others:

Say Respond

☐ ☐ I'm _____ .
☐ ☐ I'd like to introduce _____ .

I can ask and answer these questions:

Ask Answer

☐ ☐ Who is in your family?
  Who are the people in your family?
☐ ☐ What are their names?

I can talk about a photograph:

Ask Answer

☐ ☐ Who is he/she?
  Who are they?
☐ ☐ What's his/her name?
  What are their names?
☐ ☐ What's he/she doing?
  What are they doing?

STOP

Name _____

Date _____ Class _____

A IDENTIFYING & LOCATING PLACES IN THE COMMUNITY

Choose the correct answer.

1. The _____ is next to the park.
   - Ⓐ clinic
   - Ⓑ hotel
   - Ⓒ school
   - Ⓓ supermarket

3. The _____ is around the corner from the hospital.
   - Ⓐ restaurant
   - Ⓑ department store
   - Ⓒ cafeteria
   - Ⓓ supermarket

2. The laundromat is _____ the bakery and the bookstore.
   - Ⓐ across from
   - Ⓑ around the corner from
   - Ⓒ next
   - Ⓓ between

4. The library is _____ the gas station.
   - Ⓐ across from
   - Ⓑ around the corner from
   - Ⓒ next
   - Ⓓ between

B IDENTIFYING ROOMS, FURNITURE, & FIXTURES IN A RESIDENCE

5. There's a new _____ in the _____.
   - Ⓐ closet . . bedroom
   - Ⓑ refrigerator . . bathroom
   - Ⓒ stove . . kitchen
   - Ⓓ refrigerator . . kitchen

7. There's a very nice _____ in the _____.
   - Ⓐ sofa . . living room
   - Ⓑ bed . . bedroom
   - Ⓒ window . . living room
   - Ⓓ TV . . living room

6. Is there a _____ in the _____?
   - Ⓐ window . . bathroom
   - Ⓑ closet . . bedroom
   - Ⓒ closet . . living room
   - Ⓓ basement . . bedroom

8. How many _____ are there in the _____?
   - Ⓐ closets . . floor
   - Ⓑ floors . . apartment
   - Ⓒ elevators . . building
   - Ⓓ apartments . . building

- -

1 Ⓐ Ⓑ Ⓒ Ⓓ   4 Ⓐ Ⓑ Ⓒ Ⓓ   7 Ⓐ Ⓑ Ⓒ Ⓓ

2 Ⓐ Ⓑ Ⓒ Ⓓ   5 Ⓐ Ⓑ Ⓒ Ⓓ   8 Ⓐ Ⓑ Ⓒ Ⓓ

3 Ⓐ Ⓑ Ⓒ Ⓓ   6 Ⓐ Ⓑ Ⓒ Ⓓ

Go to the next page > **T19**

C GRAMMAR IN CONTEXT: Inquiring About Residences, Rentals, & Neighborhoods

Choose the correct answer to complete each conversation.

Example:

Excuse me. _____ a bank in this neighborhood?
- (A) There
- (B) Where
- (C) Are there
- (●) Is there

9. Yes. _____ a bank on State Street.
- (A) There
- (B) There's
- (C) There are
- (D) It's

10. _____
- (A) Thank.
- (B) Thanks you.
- (C) Thank you.
- (D) Yes.

11. _____
- (A) Welcome.
- (B) Yes, there is.
- (C) Thanks.
- (D) You're welcome.

12. How many bedrooms _____ in the house?
- (A) is there
- (B) are there
- (C) there is
- (D) there are

13. _____ three bedrooms.
- (A) There
- (B) There's
- (C) They are
- (D) There are

14. _____ condominiums _____ in the complex?
- (A) How . . are there
- (B) How . . there are
- (C) How many . . are there
- (D) How many . . there are

15. _____ fifty condos.
- (A) Are
- (B) There
- (C) There are
- (D) Are there

16. Is there a _____ in the apartment building?
- (A) cockroach
- (B) mailbox
- (C) satellite dish
- (D) superintendent

17. Yes. His apartment is in the _____.
- (A) basement
- (B) window
- (C) wall
- (D) roof

9 (A) (B) (C) (D)   12 (A) (B) (C) (D)   15 (A) (B) (C) (D)

10 (A) (B) (C) (D)   13 (A) (B) (C) (D)   16 (A) (B) (C) (D)

11 (A) (B) (C) (D)   14 (A) (B) (C) (D)   17 (A) (B) (C) (D)

Go to the next page ▷

Name _____ Date _____

Read and listen to the questions. Then listen to the conversation, and answer the questions.

18. How many bedrooms are there in the apartment?
- Ⓐ Six.
- Ⓑ Three.
- Ⓒ One.
- Ⓓ Two.

19. How many bathrooms are there?
- Ⓐ Six.
- Ⓑ Three.
- Ⓒ One.
- Ⓓ Two.

20. Where's the laundromat?
- Ⓐ It's next to the building.
- Ⓑ It's next to the supermarket.
- Ⓒ It's across from the building.
- Ⓓ It's across from the post office.

E SPEAKING ASSESSMENT: Information Gap (Part A)

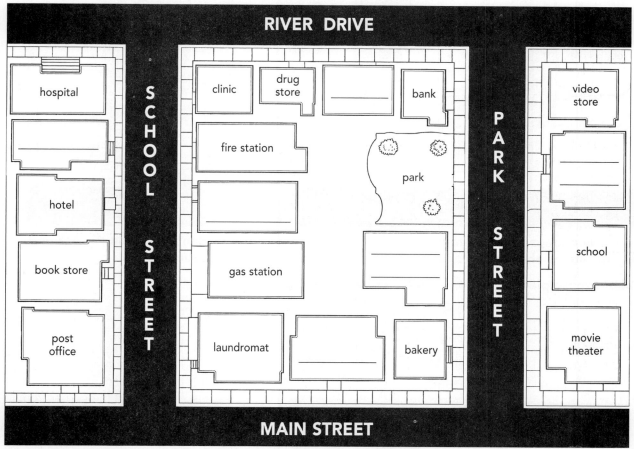

There are two maps for this activity. This is Map A. Work with a student with Map B. Ask and answer questions about the maps. Write the places in the correct locations.

Ask about these places:
- ☐ bus station
- ☐ library
- ☐ cafeteria
- ☐ department store
- ☐ supermarket
- ☐ hair salon
- ☐ restaurant

Use these expressions:
- ☐ Is there a _____ in this neighborhood?
  - ☐ Yes, there is.
  - ☐ No, there isn't.
- ☐ Where's the _____?
  - ☐ It's on _street_.
  - ☐ It's next to _____.
  - ☐ It's across from _____.
  - ☐ It's between _____.
  - ☐ It's around the corner from _____.

There are two maps for this activity. This is Map B. Work with a student with Map A. Ask and answer questions about the maps. Write the places in the correct locations.

Ask about these places:

- [ ] post office
- [ ] police station
- [ ] barber shop
- [ ] hospital
- [ ] health club
- [ ] gas station
- [ ] movie theater

Use these expressions:

- [ ] Is there a _____ in this neighborhood?
  - [ ] Yes, there is.
  - [ ] No, there isn't.

- [ ] Where's the _____?
  - [ ] It's on _street_ .
  - [ ] It's next to _____.
  - [ ] It's across from _____.
  - [ ] It's between _____.
  - [ ] It's around the corner from _____.

F WRITING ASSESSMENT

Write a paragraph about your neighborhood.

....

....

....

....

STOP

Name _____

Date _____ Class _____

8

A CLOTHING

Choose the correct answer.

Example:

I'm looking for _____.
- (A) pants
- (B) a blouse
- ● a dress
- (D) a suit

1. I'm looking for _____.

- (A) a sock
- (B) a suit
- (C) a skirt
- (D) a shirt

2. I need _____.

- (A) a shoe
- (B) a pair of shoe
- (C) a pair of shoes
- (D) pairs of shoe

3. Here's a nice _____.

- (A) tie
- (B) belt
- (C) watch
- (D) necklace

4. _____ your watch?

- (A) Are these
- (B) Are those
- (C) Is this
- (D) I think

5. _____ jeans are blue.

- (A) Those
- (B) That
- (C) This
- (D) Here's

6. Excuse me. I think that's my _____.
- (A) boots
- (B) coat
- (C) gloves
- (D) shoes

7. _____ are over there.
- (A) Sweater
- (B) Sweaters
- (C) A sock
- (D) A pair of socks

8. _____ your glasses?
- (A) Is this
- (B) Is that
- (C) Are these
- (D) Are you sure

9. _____ very nice hat!
- (A) This
- (B) That's
- (C) These are
- (D) That's a

10. Is this your jacket?
- (A) Yes, they are.
- (B) No, they aren't.
- (C) No, I'm not.
- (D) No, it isn't.

11. Excuse me. I'm looking for a gray suit.
- (A) Gray shirts are very popular.
- (B) I'm sorry. All our suits are gray.
- (C) Suits are over there.
- (D) I think this is my suit.

---

1 (A) (B) (C) (D)   4 (A) (B) (C) (D)   7 (A) (B) (C) (D)   10 (A) (B) (C) (D)

2 (A) (B) (C) (D)   5 (A) (B) (C) (D)   8 (A) (B) (C) (D)   11 (A) (B) (C) (D)

3 (A) (B) (C) (D)   6 (A) (B) (C) (D)   9 (A) (B) (C) (D)

Go to the next page **T23**

B GRAMMAR IN CONTEXT: Asking for Help • Identifying Clothing Needs

Choose the correct answer to complete the conversation.

Example:
May I help _____?
Ⓐ me
Ⓑ my
● you
Ⓓ your

12. Yes, please. I need
_____.
Ⓐ a pair of
Ⓑ glove
Ⓒ a pair of glove
Ⓓ a pair of gloves

13. Excuse me. _____
a brown umbrella.
Ⓐ I'm looking
Ⓑ I'm looking for
Ⓒ You're looking
Ⓓ You're looking for

14. I'm sorry. All our
_____ black.
Ⓐ umbrella is
Ⓑ umbrellas is
Ⓒ umbrella are
Ⓓ umbrellas are

15. Can you help _____?
Ⓐ me
Ⓑ my
Ⓒ I
Ⓓ you

Yes.

16. How much _____ coat?
Ⓐ are these
Ⓑ are those
Ⓒ is this
Ⓓ is it

17. It's very _____.
It's 25 dollars.
Ⓐ clean
Ⓑ brown
Ⓒ over there
Ⓓ inexpensive

C LISTENING ASSESSMENT

Read and listen to the questions. Then listen to the conversation, and answer the questions.

18. Where is the conversation taking place?
Ⓐ In a closet.
Ⓑ In a laundromat.
Ⓒ In a store.
Ⓓ In a restaurant.

19. What's the person looking for?
Ⓐ Her raincoat.
Ⓑ Her husband.
Ⓒ A raincoat for a man.
Ⓓ A raincoat for a woman.

20. What size is the raincoat?
Ⓐ He's tall.
Ⓑ It's large.
Ⓒ He's short.
Ⓓ It's small.

12 Ⓐ Ⓑ Ⓒ Ⓓ   15 Ⓐ Ⓑ Ⓒ Ⓓ   18 Ⓐ Ⓑ Ⓒ Ⓓ

13 Ⓐ Ⓑ Ⓒ Ⓓ   16 Ⓐ Ⓑ Ⓒ Ⓓ   19 Ⓐ Ⓑ Ⓒ Ⓓ

14 Ⓐ Ⓑ Ⓒ Ⓓ   17 Ⓐ Ⓑ Ⓒ Ⓓ   20 Ⓐ Ⓑ Ⓒ Ⓓ   Go to the next page ⟩

D MONEY: Coins

penny	nickel	dime	quarter	half-dollar
1¢	5¢	10¢	25¢	50¢
$.01	$.05	$.10	$.25	$.50

Choose the correct amount and write it.

3¢	$.05	6¢	$.10	15¢	$.20	35¢	$.50	$.61

1. _____ $.10 _____   2. _____   3. _____

4. _____   5. _____   6. _____

7. _____   8. _____   9. _____

Write the amount two ways.

10. three nickels   _____ 15¢ _____ or _____ $.15 _____

11. two pennies   _____ or _____

12. four dimes   _____ or _____

13. a quarter and a penny   _____ or _____

14. two dimes and a nickel   _____ or _____

15. a half-dollar and a dime   _____ or _____

one dollar
$1.00

five dollars
$5.00

ten dollars
$10.00

twenty dollars
$20.00

fifty dollars
$50.00

one hundred dollars
$100.00

Write the correct amount.

1. _____$25.00_____

2. _____

3. _____

4. _____

5. _____

6. _____

7. _____

8. _____

9. _____

10. _____

Go to the next page

F **CLOTHING LABELS: Sizes, Prices, Colors**

Clothing Sizes & Abbreviations

S Small   **M** Medium   **L** Large   **XL** Extra

Look at the clothing labels. Answer the questions.

221757-00-1
0001

SMALL

$30.00

1. What size is this?   _____

2. How much is it?   _____

30 **DEPT.**   27 **CLASS**   05 **SUB**

277665-700066 **SKU**

449

SIZE L
OUR PRICE **$8.99**

3. How much is this?   _____

4. What's the size?   _____

107883
H4001
WHITE
— SIZE —
36
$18.00
~~$24.00~~

5. This is on sale. What's the price?   _____

6. What size is it?   _____

7. What color is it?   _____

REGULAR FIT

BOYS

100% COTTON
CLR: BLUE

SIZE: M

$21.99

8. How big is this?   _____

9. What's the color?   _____

10. What's the cost?   _____

G CLOTHING ADS: Regular Prices, Sale Prices, Sizes

6.99 Reg. 9.99
Misses' Print Knit Tops
Assorted styles. S, M, L

14.99 Reg. 21.99
Misses' Denim Jeans
100% cotton.
Choice of Colors
Sizes 6-16

SALE 19.99

9.99 **YOUR CHOICE!** Reg. 12.99 - 17.99
Children's Athletic Shoes
Includes popular characters. Sizes & Styles vary by store.

Reg. $30.00
Men's Cotton Shirt Sizes S, M, L, XL

Look at the advertisement for clothing. Answer the questions.

1. What's the regular price of the jeans? _____

2. What's the sale price of the jeans? _____

3. How much are the children's sneakers now? _____

4. What are the sizes of the women's blouses? _____

5. What's the regular price of the men's shirts? _____

6. What's the sale price of the men's shirts? _____

7. How much are the women's blouses on sale? _____

H WRITING ASSESSMENT

What are you wearing today? Tell about the clothing and the colors. Write about it on a separate sheet of paper.

I SPEAKING ASSESSMENT

I can ask and answer these questions:

Ask Answer

☐ ☐ What are you wearing today?
☐ ☐ What color is your _clothing item_ ?
☐ ☐ What's your favorite color?

T28

Name _____

Date _____ Class _____

A COMMON ACTIVITIES

Choose the correct answer.

Example:

I _____.
- ● read
- Ⓑ reads
- Ⓒ sing
- Ⓓ sings

1. She _____ Spanish.
- Ⓐ call
- Ⓑ calls
- Ⓒ speak
- Ⓓ speaks

2. He _____ every day.
- Ⓐ cook
- Ⓑ cooks
- Ⓒ eat
- Ⓓ eats

3. They _____ in an office.
- Ⓐ live
- Ⓑ lives
- Ⓒ work
- Ⓓ works

4. He _____ TV every day.
- Ⓐ watch
- Ⓑ watches
- Ⓒ listen
- Ⓓ listens

5. She _____ to school.
- Ⓐ goes
- Ⓑ visits
- Ⓒ go
- Ⓓ visit

6. Where _____ he live?
- Ⓐ are
- Ⓑ is
- Ⓒ do
- Ⓓ does

7. What languages _____ you speak?
- Ⓐ are
- Ⓑ is
- Ⓒ do
- Ⓓ does

8. What _____ every day?
- Ⓐ do you
- Ⓑ you do
- Ⓒ do
- Ⓓ do you do

9. _____ she work?
- Ⓐ What does
- Ⓑ Where does
- Ⓒ What do
- Ⓓ Where do

10. _____ she do at the office?
- Ⓐ What does
- Ⓑ What do
- Ⓒ Where does
- Ⓓ Where do

11. _____ your parents live?
- Ⓐ What does
- Ⓑ What do
- Ⓒ Where does
- Ⓓ Where do

1 Ⓐ Ⓑ Ⓒ Ⓓ   4 Ⓐ Ⓑ Ⓒ Ⓓ   7 Ⓐ Ⓑ Ⓒ Ⓓ   10 Ⓐ Ⓑ Ⓒ Ⓓ

2 Ⓐ Ⓑ Ⓒ Ⓓ   5 Ⓐ Ⓑ Ⓒ Ⓓ   8 Ⓐ Ⓑ Ⓒ Ⓓ   11 Ⓐ Ⓑ Ⓒ Ⓓ

3 Ⓐ Ⓑ Ⓒ Ⓓ   6 Ⓐ Ⓑ Ⓒ Ⓓ   9 Ⓐ Ⓑ Ⓒ Ⓓ

Go to the next page ⟩

B GRAMMAR IN CONTEXT: Social Interactions

Choose the correct answer to complete the conversation.

12. _____ you speak?
   Ⓐ Where do
   Ⓑ Where does
   Ⓒ What language do
   Ⓓ What language does

13. I speak _____.
   Ⓐ Mexico
   Ⓑ Mexican
   Ⓒ Mexico City
   Ⓓ Spanish

14. _____ your son live?
   Ⓐ Where do
   Ⓑ Where does
   Ⓒ What do
   Ⓓ What does

15. _____ in Las Vegas.
   Ⓐ I live
   Ⓑ He lives
   Ⓒ She lives
   Ⓓ They live

16. _____ he do?
   Ⓐ What does
   Ⓑ Where does
   Ⓒ What do
   Ⓓ Where do

17. He _____ in a hotel.
   Ⓐ work
   Ⓑ works
   Ⓒ visit
   Ⓓ visits

C LISTENING ASSESSMENT

Read and listen to the questions. Then listen to the conversation, and answer the questions.

18. Where does she live?
   Ⓐ In Greece.
   Ⓑ In Dallas.
   Ⓒ In a restaurant.
   Ⓓ At work.

19. What does she do at work?
   Ⓐ She watches TV.
   Ⓑ She reads.
   Ⓒ She cooks.
   Ⓓ She plays the piano.

20. What does she do at home?
   Ⓐ She plays the violin.
   Ⓑ She reads the newspaper.
   Ⓒ She watches TV.
   Ⓓ She works.

D WRITING ASSESSMENT: Daily Activities

What do you do at home every day? What do you do at school or at work? Write about your daily activities. (Use a separate sheet of paper.)

E SPEAKING ASSESSMENT

I can ask and answer these questions:

Ask Answer
☐ ☐ What's your name?
☐ ☐ Where do you live?
☐ ☐ What languages do you speak?
☐ ☐ What do you do every day?

Ask Answer
☐ ☐ What's his/her name?
☐ ☐ Where does he/she live?
☐ ☐ What languages does he/she speak?
☐ ☐ What does he/she do every day?

12 Ⓐ Ⓑ Ⓒ Ⓓ   14 Ⓐ Ⓑ Ⓒ Ⓓ   16 Ⓐ Ⓑ Ⓒ Ⓓ   18 Ⓐ Ⓑ Ⓒ Ⓓ

13 Ⓐ Ⓑ Ⓒ Ⓓ   15 Ⓐ Ⓑ Ⓒ Ⓓ   17 Ⓐ Ⓑ Ⓒ Ⓓ   19 Ⓐ Ⓑ Ⓒ Ⓓ

20 Ⓐ Ⓑ Ⓒ Ⓓ

STOP

A COMMON ACTIVITIES: DAILY LIFE, SPORTS, & RECREATION

Choose the best answer.

Example:

Tom _____ basketball on Saturday. He plays basketball on Friday.
- Ⓐ play
- Ⓑ doesn't play
- Ⓒ don't play
- Ⓓ not play   Ⓐ ● Ⓒ Ⓓ

1. My wife and I _____ on Sunday. We go to a restaurant.
   - Ⓐ don't cook
   - Ⓑ doesn't cook
   - Ⓒ don't we cook
   - Ⓓ not cook

2. _____ Janet play tennis on Monday?
   - Ⓐ Is
   - Ⓑ Do
   - Ⓒ Don't
   - Ⓓ Does

3. _____ your parents watch TV?
   - Ⓐ Does
   - Ⓑ Are
   - Ⓒ Do
   - Ⓓ What

4. Does Mr. Lee ride his bike to work?
   - Ⓐ Yes, they do.
   - Ⓑ Yes, it does.
   - Ⓒ Yes, I do.
   - Ⓓ Yes, he does.

5. Do you and your friends play baseball?
   - Ⓐ Yes, we do.
   - Ⓑ Yes, they do.
   - Ⓒ Yes, he does.
   - Ⓓ Yes, it does.

6. Do you play a musical instrument?
   - Ⓐ Yes, they do.
   - Ⓑ Yes, you do.
   - Ⓒ No, I don't.
   - Ⓓ No, it doesn't.

7. What do your friends do on the weekend?
   - Ⓐ Yes, we do.
   - Ⓑ Yes, they do.
   - Ⓒ They play football.
   - Ⓓ I play football.

8. _____ movies do you like?
   - Ⓐ What kind
   - Ⓑ What kind of
   - Ⓒ What's your favorite
   - Ⓓ Who's your favorite

9. My parents _____ go to concerts because my father _____ like classical music.
   - Ⓐ don't . . don't
   - Ⓑ doesn't . . doesn't
   - Ⓒ doesn't . . don't
   - Ⓓ don't . . doesn't

10. My brother _____ very popular. He _____ to a lot of parties.
    - Ⓐ is . . go
    - Ⓑ does . . go
    - Ⓒ is . . goes
    - Ⓓ does . . goes

11. I _____ comedies, and my sister _____ dramas.
    - Ⓐ like . . like
    - Ⓑ like . . likes
    - Ⓒ likes . . likes
    - Ⓓ likes . . like

....

1 Ⓐ Ⓑ Ⓒ Ⓓ   4 Ⓐ Ⓑ Ⓒ Ⓓ   7 Ⓐ Ⓑ Ⓒ Ⓓ   10 Ⓐ Ⓑ Ⓒ Ⓓ

2 Ⓐ Ⓑ Ⓒ Ⓓ   5 Ⓐ Ⓑ Ⓒ Ⓓ   8 Ⓐ Ⓑ Ⓒ Ⓓ   11 Ⓐ Ⓑ Ⓒ Ⓓ

3 Ⓐ Ⓑ Ⓒ Ⓓ   6 Ⓐ Ⓑ Ⓒ Ⓓ   9 Ⓐ Ⓑ Ⓒ Ⓓ

B GRAMMAR IN CONTEXT: Ordering in a Fast Food Restaurant

Read the story. Then choose the correct answer to complete each conversation.

MONDAY	TUESDAY	WEDNESDAY	THURSDAY	FRIDAY	SATURDAY	SUNDAY

Fran's Fast Food Restaurant is a very special place. Every day Fran cooks a different kind of fast food. On Monday she cooks hamburgers. On Tuesday she cooks cheeseburgers. On Wednesday she makes tacos. On Thursday she makes pizza. On Friday she cooks chicken. On Saturday she cooks hot dogs. And on Sunday she makes sandwiches.

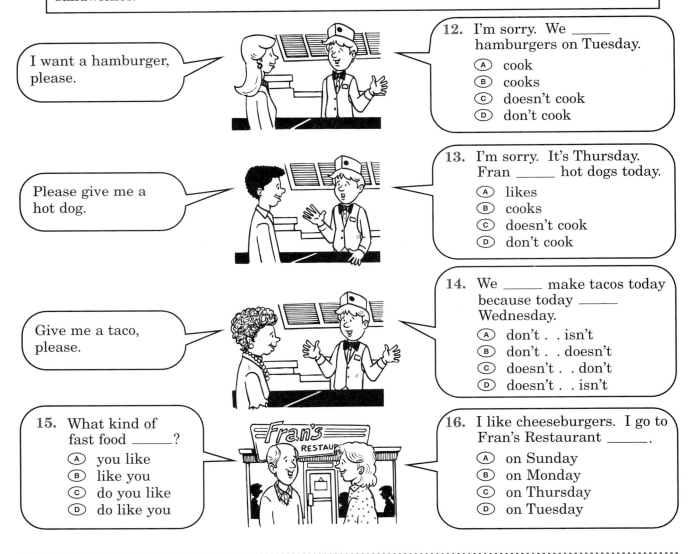

I want a hamburger, please.

12. I'm sorry. We _____ hamburgers on Tuesday.
   A cook
   B cooks
   C doesn't cook
   D don't cook

Please give me a hot dog.

13. I'm sorry. It's Thursday. Fran _____ hot dogs today.
   A likes
   B cooks
   C doesn't cook
   D don't cook

Give me a taco, please.

14. We _____ make tacos today because today _____ Wednesday.
   A don't . . isn't
   B don't . . doesn't
   C doesn't . . don't
   D doesn't . . isn't

15. What kind of fast food _____?
   A you like
   B like you
   C do you like
   D do like you

16. I like cheeseburgers. I go to Fran's Restaurant _____.
   A on Sunday
   B on Monday
   C on Thursday
   D on Tuesday

12 Ⓐ Ⓑ Ⓒ Ⓓ   14 Ⓐ Ⓑ Ⓒ Ⓓ   16 Ⓐ Ⓑ Ⓒ Ⓓ

13 Ⓐ Ⓑ Ⓒ Ⓓ   15 Ⓐ Ⓑ Ⓒ Ⓓ

Go to the next page ▷

C LISTENING ASSESSMENT

Read and listen to the questions. Then listen to the story, and answer the questions.

17. What do they do on Tuesday?
   - (A) They jog.
   - (B) They play tennis.
   - (C) They play golf.
   - (D) They play basketball.

18. Do they ride their bikes on Wednesday?
   - (A) Yes, he does.
   - (B) Yes, she does.
   - (C) Yes, they do.
   - (D) No, they don't.

19. What do they do on Friday?
   - (A) They play golf.
   - (B) They play basketball.
   - (C) He plays golf, and she plays basketball.
   - (D) She plays golf, and he plays basketball.

20. What do they do on the weekend?
   - (A) She does yoga, and he swims.
   - (B) They jog.
   - (C) They go to a health club.
   - (D) They're very athletic people.

D WRITING & GRAMMAR ASSESSMENT

Write the correct words to complete the sentences.

1. I ___live___ in New York.   He ___lives___ in Los Angeles.

2. I _____ in a bank.   She _____ in an office.

3. I _____ a taxi.   He _____ a bus.

4. I _____ the piano.   She _____ the violin.

5. I _____ the newspaper.   He _____ books.

6. I _____ to movies.   She _____ to concerts.

7. I _____ English.   He _____ Spanish.

8. I _____ TV.   She _____ videos.

E WRITING ASSESSMENT: Days of the Week

Look at the abbreviation. Write the correct day of the week.

MON _____Monday_____   THU _____

FRI _____   SUN _____

TUE _____   WED _____

SAT _____

F WRITING ASSESSMENT: Recreation & Entertainment Activities

What do you do on the weekend? How do you spend your time? Write a paragraph about it.

....

....

....

....

....

....

G SPEAKING ASSESSMENT

I can ask and answer these questions:

Ask Answer
☐ ☐ What do you do during the week?
☐ ☐ What do you do on the weekend?

☐ ☐ Do you like _Italian/ Greek / Chinese / Puerto Rican / Japanese / Mexican / American_ food?
☐ ☐ What kind of food do you like?

☐ ☐ Do you like _comedies / dramas / westerns / adventure movies / science fiction movies / cartoons_?
☐ ☐ What kind of movies do you like?

☐ ☐ Do you like _novels / poetry / short stories / non-fiction / biographies_?
☐ ☐ What kind of books do you like?

☐ ☐ Do you like _comedies / dramas / cartoons / game shows / news programs_?
☐ ☐ What kind of TV programs do you like?

☐ ☐ Do you like _classical music / popular music / jazz / rock music / country music_?
☐ ☐ What kind of music do you like?

☐ ☐ Do you like _football / baseball / soccer / golf / hockey / tennis_?
☐ ☐ What kind of sports do you like?

STOP

A FAMILY RELATIONS

Choose the correct answer.

1. My grandparents live in Chicago. We call
   _____ every Sunday.
   - (A) him
   - (B) her
   - (C) us
   - (D) them

2. My uncle is in the hospital. My aunt
   visits _____ there every day.
   - (A) him
   - (B) her
   - (C) me
   - (D) them

3. Our son's wife is very nice. We like _____
   very much.
   - (A) it
   - (B) him
   - (C) her
   - (D) them

4. My father usually washes his car on
   Thursday. He rarely washes _____ on
   Friday.
   - (A) her
   - (B) him
   - (C) it
   - (D) them

5. We talk to our daughter every weekend.
   She always calls _____ on Saturday.
   - (A) him
   - (B) us
   - (C) we
   - (D) her

6. You're my very close friend. I think
   about _____ all the time.
   - (A) me
   - (B) your
   - (C) you
   - (D) them

7. My sister always studies in the library.
   She _____ studies in her room.
   - (A) always
   - (B) usually
   - (C) sometimes
   - (D) never

8. My parents _____ a small apartment.
   - (A) has
   - (B) live
   - (C) in
   - (D) have

9. Their son _____ brown hair.
   - (A) has
   - (B) have
   - (C) is
   - (D) his

10. Our neighbors _____ a new satellite dish.
    - (A) are
    - (B) never
    - (C) has
    - (D) have

11. I _____ one sister. My sister _____ blue
    eyes.
    - (A) have . . have
    - (B) has . . have
    - (C) have . . has
    - (D) have . . is

12. My brother _____ curly hair. My sisters
    _____ straight hair.
    - (A) have . . have
    - (B) has . . have
    - (C) have . . has
    - (D) has . . has

1 (A)(B)(C)(D) 4 (A)(B)(C)(D) 7 (A)(B)(C)(D) 10 (A)(B)(C)(D)
2 (A)(B)(C)(D) 5 (A)(B)(C)(D) 8 (A)(B)(C)(D) 11 (A)(B)(C)(D)
3 (A)(B)(C)(D) 6 (A)(B)(C)(D) 9 (A)(B)(C)(D) 12 (A)(B)(C)(D)

Go to the next page

B GRAMMAR IN CONTEXT: Asking for Tableware • Describing Oneself

Choose the correct answer to complete the conversation.

> Excuse me. I need a fork and knife, please.

14. Yes. _____ a spoon for my granddaughter?
- (A) You have
- (B) Do you have
- (C) You do have
- (D) Do have

> Yes. Always.

16. _____ look like?
- (A) Who you
- (B) Who do you
- (C) Do you
- (D) How often do you

13. Here you are. _____ eat pizza with a fork and knife?
- (A) You usually
- (B) You do usually
- (C) Do you usually
- (D) Do usually

15. Yes. _____ eat spaghetti with a spoon?
- (A) Always
- (B) She always
- (C) Is she always
- (D) Does she always

17. I look like my brother. We both have _____ hair.
- (A) tall
- (B) heavy
- (C) brown
- (D) different

C LISTENING ASSESSMENT

Read and listen to the questions. Then listen to the story, and answer the questions.

18. How does this person look like her sister?
- (A) They're both short.
- (B) They both have brown eyes.
- (C) They both have long hair.
- (D) They both have brown hair.

19. Where does the teacher live?
- (A) In the suburbs.
- (B) In the city.
- (C) In a small apartment.
- (D) In a school.

20. What do they do every day?
- (A) They watch videos.
- (B) They talk on the telephone.
- (C) They go to parties.
- (D) They're very different.

D WRITING ASSESSMENT

Write about yourself and another person. Do you look like this person? Describe how you and this person are different. (Use a separate sheet of paper.)

E SPEAKING ASSESSMENT

I can ask and answer these questions:

Ask Answer
- ☐ ☐ Do you have any brothers or sisters?
- ☐ ☐ Tell me about your family. (I have . . .)

- ☐ ☐ Tell me about a family member or a friend:
- ☐ ☐ What's his/her name?
- ☐ ☐ What does he/she look like?
- ☐ ☐ What does he/she do?

13 (A) (B) (C) (D)   15 (A) (B) (C) (D)   17 (A) (B) (C) (D)   19 (A) (B) (C) (D)
14 (A) (B) (C) (D)   16 (A) (B) (C) (D)   18 (A) (B) (C) (D)   20 (A) (B) (C) (D)

STOP

A DESCRIBING STATES OF BEING

1. Is he happy?
   Ⓐ No. He's tired.
   Ⓑ No. He's angry.
   Ⓒ No. He's sad.
   Ⓓ No. He's nervous.

2. Is she hungry?
   Ⓐ No. She's happy.
   Ⓑ No. She's thirsty.
   Ⓒ No. She's cold.
   Ⓓ No. She's scared.

3. Is he tired?
   Ⓐ No. He's scared.
   Ⓑ No. He's sick.
   Ⓒ No. He's hungry.
   Ⓓ No. He's angry.

4. Are they cold?
   Ⓐ Yes. They cry.
   Ⓑ Yes. They're crying.
   Ⓒ Yes. They shiver.
   Ⓓ Yes. They're shivering.

5. Why are you perspiring?
   Ⓐ I'm cold.
   Ⓑ I'm happy.
   Ⓒ I'm hot.
   Ⓓ I'm angry.

6. What do you do when you're tired?
   Ⓐ I yawn.
   Ⓑ I'm yawning.
   Ⓒ We're smiling.
   Ⓓ You shout.

7. _____ when I'm nervous.
   Ⓐ I'm blushing
   Ⓑ I'm perspiring
   Ⓒ I'm biting my nails
   Ⓓ I always bite my nails

8. _____ because she's happy today.
   Ⓐ She smiles
   Ⓑ She's smiling
   Ⓒ She always smiles
   Ⓓ She never smiles

B GRAMMAR IN CONTEXT: Asking About Home Activities

9. _____ doing?
   Ⓐ What do you
   Ⓑ What are you
   Ⓒ Why do you
   Ⓓ Why are you

10. _____ the rug with a broom.
    Ⓐ I sweep
    Ⓑ I walk
    Ⓒ I'm sweeping
    Ⓓ I'm walking

11. _____ the rug with a broom?
    Ⓐ Are you usually walking
    Ⓑ Are you usually sleeping
    Ⓒ Do you usually walk
    Ⓓ Do you usually sweep

12. No. My _____ is broken.
    Ⓐ vacuum
    Ⓑ flashlight
    Ⓒ hammer
    Ⓓ computer

1 Ⓐ Ⓑ Ⓒ Ⓓ   4 Ⓐ Ⓑ Ⓒ Ⓓ   7 Ⓐ Ⓑ Ⓒ Ⓓ   10 Ⓐ Ⓑ Ⓒ Ⓓ
2 Ⓐ Ⓑ Ⓒ Ⓓ   5 Ⓐ Ⓑ Ⓒ Ⓓ   8 Ⓐ Ⓑ Ⓒ Ⓓ   11 Ⓐ Ⓑ Ⓒ Ⓓ
3 Ⓐ Ⓑ Ⓒ Ⓓ   6 Ⓐ Ⓑ Ⓒ Ⓓ   9 Ⓐ Ⓑ Ⓒ Ⓓ   12 Ⓐ Ⓑ Ⓒ Ⓓ

Go to the next page

C READING

Read the story. Then answer the questions.

> It isn't a typical Monday morning at the Lane family's apartment. Mr. Lane usually takes the train to his laboratory, but he isn't taking the train today. Mrs. Lane usually drives to her office, but she isn't driving there today. Jimmy and Jennifer Lane usually take the bus to school, but they aren't taking the bus today. And Julie Lane usually rides her bicycle to her job at the shopping mall, but she isn't riding her bicycle there today. It's snowing very hard this morning. The streets are empty, and the city is quiet. Everybody in town is staying home.

13. Who usually goes to work in a car?
- Ⓐ Mr. Lane.
- Ⓑ Mrs. Lane.
- Ⓒ Jimmy Lane.
- Ⓓ Julie Lane.

14. How do the young children in the family usually go to school?
- Ⓐ They take the train.
- Ⓑ They're taking the train.
- Ⓒ They take the bus.
- Ⓓ They're taking the bus.

15. Who works in a store?
- Ⓐ Mr. Lane.
- Ⓑ Mrs. Lane.
- Ⓒ Jennifer Lane.
- Ⓓ Julie Lane.

16. Why is everybody in town staying home this morning?
- Ⓐ The streets are empty.
- Ⓑ The city is quiet.
- Ⓒ It's snowing.
- Ⓓ It's cold.

D LISTENING ASSESSMENT

Read and listen to the questions. Then listen to the conversation, and answer the questions.

17. What does Wanda do at the office?
- Ⓐ She answers the telephone.
- Ⓑ She sorts the mail.
- Ⓒ She cleans the office.
- Ⓓ She types all the letters.

18. Who cleans the office?
- Ⓐ Ken.
- Ⓑ Mrs. Kent.
- Ⓒ George.
- Ⓓ Nancy.

19. What's Nancy's job?
- Ⓐ She's sick today.
- Ⓑ She's at home with the flu.
- Ⓒ She usually types letters.
- Ⓓ She's typing letters today.

20. Where's Mrs. Kent?
- Ⓐ She's with the president.
- Ⓑ She's at home with the flu.
- Ⓒ She's the boss.
- Ⓓ She's at the dentist.

E WRITING ASSESSMENT: States of Being

What do you usually do when you're happy? sad? tired? hungry? thirsty? Write about it on a separate sheet of paper.

F SPEAKING ASSESSMENT

I can ask and answer these questions:

Ask Answer
- ☐ ☐ Are you hungry?
- ☐ ☐ Are you thirsty?
- ☐ ☐ Are you _happy/sad/tired_?
- ☐ ☐ Why are you _happy/sad/tired_?

Ask Answer
- ☐ ☐ How do you go to school?
- ☐ ☐ Do you drive a car?
- ☐ ☐ Do you take a bus/train?
- ☐ ☐ Do you walk?
- ☐ ☐ Do you ride a bicycle?

....

13 Ⓐ Ⓑ Ⓒ Ⓓ   15 Ⓐ Ⓑ Ⓒ Ⓓ   17 Ⓐ Ⓑ Ⓒ Ⓓ   19 Ⓐ Ⓑ Ⓒ Ⓓ

14 Ⓐ Ⓑ Ⓒ Ⓓ   16 Ⓐ Ⓑ Ⓒ Ⓓ   18 Ⓐ Ⓑ Ⓒ Ⓓ   20 Ⓐ Ⓑ Ⓒ Ⓓ

● T38

A OCCUPATIONS, ABILITIES, & SKILLS

1. What's his job?
   - (A) He's a teacher.
   - (B) He's a singer.
   - (C) He's a baker.
   - (D) He's an actor.

2. What's her occupation?
   - (A) She's a dancer.
   - (B) She's a chef.
   - (C) She's a secretary.
   - (D) She's a mechanic.

3. Can he type?
   Yes. He's _____.
   - (A) a superintendent
   - (B) a secretary
   - (C) a salesperson
   - (D) a computer

4. What can you do?
   I can _____.
   - (A) use a cash register
   - (B) use a calculator
   - (C) use business software
   - (D) use a computer

5. I can cook.
   - (A) I'm a construction worker.
   - (B) I'm a chef.
   - (C) I'm a mechanic.
   - (D) I'm a driver.

6. She can talk to customers.
   - (A) She's a teacher.
   - (B) She's a singer.
   - (C) She's a salesperson.
   - (D) She's a dancer.

7. He can build things.
   - (A) He's a mechanic.
   - (B) He's a salesperson.
   - (C) He's a building superintendent.
   - (D) He's a construction worker.

8. Tell me about your skills.
   - (A) I'm looking for work.
   - (B) I'm looking for a job as a secretary.
   - (C) I can file and type.
   - (D) I'm a salesperson.

B GRAMMAR IN CONTEXT: Requesting Permission to Leave Work • Calling to Explain Absence

9. May I leave work early today?
   _____ go to the doctor.
   - (A) You have
   - (B) You have to
   - (C) I have
   - (D) I have to

10. Okay. _____ leave early.
    - (A) You have to
    - (B) You can
    - (C) I have to
    - (D) I can

11. I'm sorry. _____ come to work today. I'm sick.
    - (A) You can
    - (B) I can
    - (C) I can't
    - (D) I have to

12. That's okay. _____ come to work.
    - (A) Don't have to
    - (B) You don't have to
    - (C) I have to
    - (D) I don't have to

1 (A) (B) (C) (D)   4 (A) (B) (C) (D)   7 (A) (B) (C) (D)   10 (A) (B) (C) (D)

2 (A) (B) (C) (D)   5 (A) (B) (C) (D)   8 (A) (B) (C) (D)   11 (A) (B) (C) (D)

3 (A) (B) (C) (D)   6 (A) (B) (C) (D)   9 (A) (B) (C) (D)   12 (A) (B) (C) (D)

Go to the next page ➔

C READING: "Help Wanted" Sign

Read the sign. Then answer the questions.

> ### NOW HIRING!
> - Looking for new employees.
> - Days or eves
> - FT & PT
> - $9.00 / hr.
>   Ask cashier in store for application form

13. What's the salary?
- (A) Nine dollars per week.
- (B) Nine dollars per month.
- (C) Nine dollars per hour.
- (D) Nine dollars per year.

14. What kind of jobs are there?
- (A) Only jobs during the day.
- (B) Only jobs during the evening.
- (C) Only jobs for cashiers.
- (D) Full-time jobs and part-time jobs.

15. What does a person have to do to apply for a job there?
- (A) Fill out an application form.
- (B) Work days and evenings.
- (C) Look for new employees.
- (D) Talk with the president of the company.

D READING: Classified Ads

Read the job advertisements. Then answer the questions.

HELP WANTED
BAKER
Small bakery. M–F. Full-time. Apply in person. G&R Pastry Shop. 700 Central Ave.
Secretary
Large office. Call Mary at 262-7910.
CASHIERS
Large supermarket. FT & PT. Days & eves. 420 Main St. Apply in person. Ask for Ray.

16. Chet can type and file. He's applying for a job. What does he have to do?
- (A) He has to go to 700 Central Avenue.
- (B) He has to go to 420 Main Street.
- (C) He has to talk with Ray.
- (D) He has to call 262-7910.

17. Sheila can use a cash register. She's applying for a job. What does she have to do?
- (A) She has to work full-time.
- (B) She has to go to 420 Main Street.
- (C) She has to call Mary.
- (D) She has to work part-time.

E LISTENING ASSESSMENT

Read and listen to the questions. Then listen to the job interview, and answer the questions.

18. Where is the job interview taking place?
- (A) In a restaurant.
- (B) In a bank.
- (C) In a store.
- (D) In a computer company.

19. What can David do?
- (A) He can paint.
- (B) He can take inventory.
- (C) He can teach.
- (D) He can use tools.

20. David doesn't have one skill. What <u>can't</u> he do?
- (A) Take inventory.
- (B) Use a cash register.
- (C) Talk to customers.
- (D) Operate business software.

13 (A) (B) (C) (D)   15 (A) (B) (C) (D)   17 (A) (B) (C) (D)   19 (A) (B) (C) (D)

14 (A) (B) (C) (D)   16 (A) (B) (C) (D)   18 (A) (B) (C) (D)   20 (A) (B) (C) (D)

Go to the next page ⟩

F WRITING: Job Application Form

Complete this form about yourself.

Name: _____ Social Security No. _____

Street: _____ Apartment: _____

City: _____ State: _____ Zip Code: _____

Telephone: _____

Skills and Abilities:

What can you do? Describe your skills and abilities:

_____

_____

_____

Work Experience:

Job	Company	From	To
_____	_____	_____	_____
_____	_____	_____	_____
_____	_____	_____	_____
_____	_____	_____	_____

Education:

School	City, State	From	To
_____	_____	_____	_____
_____	_____	_____	_____
_____	_____	_____	_____
_____	_____	_____	_____

Date: _____ Signature: _____

G POLICE/SAFETY COMMANDS & SIGNS

For each command, choose the correct sign.

A

B

C

D

E

F

1. "Danger! Don't stand there!" _____

2. "Danger! Don't touch that!" _____

3. "Wear a helmet!" _____

4. "Wear safety glasses!" _____

5. "Don't go that way!" _____

6. "Halt! Freeze! Don't move!" _____

H SPEAKING ASSESSMENT

I can ask and answer these questions about job skills and other abilities:

Ask Answer

☐ ☐ Can you __job skill__?
☐ ☐ What can you do? Tell me about your skills.

☐ ☐ Can you play __sport__?
☐ ☐ What sports can you play?

☐ ☐ Can you play __musical instrument__?
☐ ☐ What musical instrument can you play?

Ask Answer

☐ ☐ Can you speak __language__?
☐ ☐ What languages can you speak?

☐ ☐ Can you cook?
☐ ☐ What can you cook?

STOP

Name _____

Date _____ **Class** _____

A TIME

1. It's _____.
   Ⓐ 7:00
   Ⓑ 8:00
   Ⓒ 6:30
   Ⓓ 7:30

2. It's _____.
   Ⓐ 11:15
   Ⓑ 11:45
   Ⓒ 9:00
   Ⓓ 9:45

3. It's _____.
   Ⓐ a quarter to five
   Ⓑ half past six
   Ⓒ half past five
   Ⓓ a quarter to six

4. The time is _____.
   Ⓐ a quarter to three
   Ⓑ a quarter to four
   Ⓒ half past three
   Ⓓ half past four

5. What's the weather forecast for tomorrow?
   Ⓐ It rains.
   Ⓑ It's raining.
   Ⓒ It's going to rain.
   Ⓓ I'm going to go to the beach.

6. What are you going to do tomorrow?
   Ⓐ We're going to clean our apartment.
   Ⓑ He's going to cook.
   Ⓒ It's going to be cloudy.
   Ⓓ They're going to have a picnic.

7. What time does the train leave?
   Ⓐ It begins at 6:00.
   Ⓑ It's 6:00.
   Ⓒ It's going to leave.
   Ⓓ At 6:00.

8. What's the date?
   Ⓐ It's 4:00.
   Ⓑ It's Thursday.
   Ⓒ It's April 10th.
   Ⓓ It's spring.

B GRAMMAR IN CONTEXT: Asking & Telling Time • Congratulating

9. _____ is it?
   Ⓐ What time
   Ⓑ What's the time
   Ⓒ Tell the time
   Ⓓ Tell me the time

10. _____
    Ⓐ It's sunny and warm.
    Ⓑ It's two o'clock.
    Ⓒ I'm going to study.
    Ⓓ It's November 4th.

11. _____ August 31st. Today is my birthday!
    Ⓐ Today
    Ⓑ It
    Ⓒ It's
    Ⓓ I'm

12. Congratulations! _____
    Ⓐ Oh no!
    Ⓑ Happy New Year!
    Ⓒ Happy Thanksgiving!
    Ⓓ Happy Birthday!

1 Ⓐ Ⓑ Ⓒ Ⓓ   4 Ⓐ Ⓑ Ⓒ Ⓓ   7 Ⓐ Ⓑ Ⓒ Ⓓ   10 Ⓐ Ⓑ Ⓒ Ⓓ
2 Ⓐ Ⓑ Ⓒ Ⓓ   5 Ⓐ Ⓑ Ⓒ Ⓓ   8 Ⓐ Ⓑ Ⓒ Ⓓ   11 Ⓐ Ⓑ Ⓒ Ⓓ
3 Ⓐ Ⓑ Ⓒ Ⓓ   6 Ⓐ Ⓑ Ⓒ Ⓓ   9 Ⓐ Ⓑ Ⓒ Ⓓ   12 Ⓐ Ⓑ Ⓒ Ⓓ

Go to the next page →

C READING: National Holidays in the United States & Canada

Read the story. Then answer the questions.

> Some holidays in the United States and Canada are on the same date every year. New Year's Day is always on January 1st. Christmas Day is always on December 25th. Canadians always celebrate Canada Day on July 1st, and people in the United States always celebrate Independence Day on July 4th. Veterans Day in the U.S. and Remembrance Day in Canada are always on November 11th.
>
> Other holidays are on different dates every year because these holidays are on certain days of the week. For example, in the U.S. and Canada, Labor Day is always on the first Monday in September. Thanksgiving Day in the U.S. is always on the fourth Thursday in November. In Canada, Thanksgiving Day is on the second Monday in October. Many other U.S. holidays are always on Monday: Martin Luther King, Jr. Day in January, Presidents' Day in February, Memorial Day in May, and Columbus Day in October.

13. Which holiday is in September?
    - Ⓐ Presidents' Day.
    - Ⓑ Memorial Day.
    - Ⓒ Columbus Day.
    - Ⓓ Labor Day.

14. Which holiday is always on the same date every year?
    - Ⓐ Thanksgiving Day.
    - Ⓑ Labor Day.
    - Ⓒ New Year's Day.
    - Ⓓ Memorial Day.

15. Which sentence is correct?
    - Ⓐ New Year's Day is always on Monday.
    - Ⓑ Memorial Day in the U.S. is always on Monday.
    - Ⓒ Canada Day is in June.
    - Ⓓ Christmas Day is on December 24th.

16. Which sentence is not correct?
    - Ⓐ Canada and the U.S. celebrate Labor Day on the same day.
    - Ⓑ Canada and the U.S. have a holiday on November 11th.
    - Ⓒ New Year's Day is on the first day of January.
    - Ⓓ Canada and the U.S. celebrate Thanksgiving on the same day.

D LISTENING ASSESSMENT

Read and listen to the questions. Then listen to the story, and answer the questions.

17. What's he going to do in March?
    - Ⓐ He's going to start a new job.
    - Ⓑ He's going to move.
    - Ⓒ He's going to get married.
    - Ⓓ He's going to have a birthday party.

18. When is he going to begin to study at a computer school?
    - Ⓐ In January.
    - Ⓑ In June.
    - Ⓒ In September.
    - Ⓓ In December.

19. Where is he going to work?
    - Ⓐ In an office.
    - Ⓑ In a new apartment building.
    - Ⓒ In a computer school.
    - Ⓓ In Honolulu.

20. How old is he going to be in June?
    - Ⓐ 13 years old.
    - Ⓑ 23 years old.
    - Ⓒ 30 years old.
    - Ⓓ 40 years old.

13 Ⓐ Ⓑ Ⓒ Ⓓ   16 Ⓐ Ⓑ Ⓒ Ⓓ   19 Ⓐ Ⓑ Ⓒ Ⓓ

14 Ⓐ Ⓑ Ⓒ Ⓓ   17 Ⓐ Ⓑ Ⓒ Ⓓ   20 Ⓐ Ⓑ Ⓒ Ⓓ

● **T44**   15 Ⓐ Ⓑ Ⓒ Ⓓ   18 Ⓐ Ⓑ Ⓒ Ⓓ   Go to the next page ⟩

E THE CALENDAR

2009

January

S	M	T	W	T	F	S
				1	2	3	4
5	6	7	8	9	10	11
12	13	14	15	16	17	18
19	20	21	22	23	24	25
26	27	28	29	30	31	

February

S	M	T	W	T	F	S
						1
2	3	4	5	6	7	8
9	10	11	12	13	14	15
16	17	18	19	20	21	22
23	24	25	26	27	28	

March

S	M	T	W	T	F	S
1						
2	3	4	5	6	7	8
9	10	11	12	13	14	15
16	17	18	19	20	21	22
23/30	24/31	25	26	27	28	29

April

S	M	T	W	T	F	S
			1	2	3	4	5
6	7	8	9	10	11	12
13	14	15	16	17	18	19
20	21	22	23	24	25	26
27	28	29	30			

May

S	M	T	W	T	F	S
					1	2	3
4	5	6	7	8	9	10
11	12	13	14	15	16	17
18	19	20	21	22	23	24
25	26	27	28	29	30	31

June

S	M	T	W	T	F	S
	1	2	3	4	5	6	7
8	9	10	11	12	13	14
15	16	17	18	19	20	21
22	23	24	25	26	27	28
29	30					

July

S	M	T	W	T	F	S
			1	2	3	4	5
6	7	8	9	10	11	12
13	14	15	16	17	18	19
20	21	22	23	24	25	26
27	28	29	30	31		

August

S	M	T	W	T	F	S
						1	2
3	4	5	6	7	8	9
10	11	12	13	14	15	16
17	18	19	20	21	22	23
24/31	25	26	27	28	29	30

September

S	M	T	W	T	F	S
		1	2	3	4	5	6
7	8	9	10	11	12	13
14	15	16	17	18	19	20
21	22	23	24	25	26	27
28	29	30				

October

S	M	T	W	T	F	S
				1	2	3	4
5	6	7	8	9	10	11
12	13	14	15	16	17	18
19	20	21	22	23	24	25
26	27	28	29	30	31	

November

S	M	T	W	T	F	S
1						
2	3	4	5	6	7	8
9	10	11	12	13	14	15
16	17	18	19	20	21	22
23/30	24	25	26	27	28	29

December

S	M	T	W	T	F	S
	1	2	3	4	5	6
7	8	9	10	11	12	13
14	15	16	17	18	19	20
21	22	23	24	25	26	27
28	29	30	31			

Circle these dates on the calendar.

March 7	June 2nd
September 25	5/13/09
April 15th	8/20/09
January 23rd	10/31/09

On this calendar, what day of the week is . . .

July 4th	_____Friday_____	11/16/09	_____
February 10th	_____	1/14/09	_____
May 22nd	_____	3/5/09	_____

F ORDINAL NUMBERS

1st	11th	21st
2nd	12th	22nd
3rd	13th	23rd
4th	14th	24th
5th	15th	25th
6th	16th	26th
7th	17th	27th
8th	18th	28th
9th	19th	29th
10th	20th	30th

Write the correct ordinal number.

third	_____	seventh	_____
fifteenth	_____	twenty-first	_____
second	_____	twelfth	_____
thirtieth	_____	eighteenth	_____

G WRITING ASSESSMENT: Months of the Year

Look at the abbreviation. Write the correct month of the year.

MAR _____	DEC _____	APR _____
AUG _____	FEB _____	JUN _____
NOV _____	JAN _____	MAY _____
SEP _____	OCT _____	JUL _____

H CLOCK TIMES

_2:00_ _____ _____ _____ _____ _____

I WRITING ASSESSMENT: Fill Out the Forms

First Name: _____   Last Name: _____

Date of Birth: _____   Place of Birth: _____

Signature: _____   Today's Date: _____

Last Name: | | | | | | | | | | | | | | First Name: | | | | | | | | | | | | | | | |

Date of Birth: |__|__|__| Today's Date: |__|__|__| Signature: [   ]
       Month Day Year   Month Day Year

J WRITING ASSESSMENT: Day & Date

What day is it? ....

What's today's date? ....

K WRITING ASSESSMENT: Future Plans

What are you going to do tomorrow? Tell about five or more things you are going to do. Use a separate sheet of paper.

L SPEAKING ASSESSMENT

I can ask and answer questions about dates, time, and weather:

Ask Answer
☐ ☐ What day is it today?
☐ ☐ What's today's date?
What's the date today?

Ask Answer
☐ ☐ What day is it tomorrow?
☐ ☐ What's tomorrow's date?

Ask Answer
☐ ☐ What time is it?
☐ ☐ What's your birthdate?
☐ ☐ What's the weather forecast for tomorrow?

I can ask and answer questions about common activities and time:

Ask Answer
What time do you usually . . .
☐ ☐ get up?
☐ ☐ eat breakfast?
☐ ☐ go to school?
☐ ☐ eat lunch?
☐ ☐ eat dinner?
☐ ☐ go to bed?

Ask Answer
What time are you going to . . .
☐ ☐ get up tomorrow?
☐ ☐ eat breakfast tomorrow?
☐ ☐ go to school tomorrow?
☐ ☐ eat lunch tomorrow?
☐ ☐ eat dinner tomorrow?
☐ ☐ go to bed tomorrow?

15

A MEDICAL CARE: Parts of the Body & Ailments

Choose the correct answer.

Example:

Her _____ hurts. She has _____.
- (A) throat . . a sore throat
- (B) ear . . an earache
- ● head . . a headache
- (D) tooth . . a toothache

1. Her _____ hurts. She has _____.
- (A) back . . a backache
- (B) ear . . an earache
- (C) stomach . . a stomachache
- (D) throat . . a sore throat

2. He has _____. He wants some _____.
- (A) a fever . . cold
- (B) a toothache . . candy
- (C) a cold . . hot dogs
- (D) a cold . . cold medicine

3. He has _____. He wants some _____.
- (A) a cough . . cough syrup
- (B) a stomachache . . antacid tablets
- (C) an earache . . ear drops
- (D) a headache . . aspirin

4. Betsy has a stomachache because she _____ all day yesterday.
- (A) eats cookies
- (B) ate cookies
- (C) rests
- (D) rested

5. Robert has a backache because he _____ all day.
- (A) talked
- (B) sang
- (C) planted flowers
- (D) cried

6. Peggy has a sore throat because she _____ all day.
- (A) shouted
- (B) listened to loud music
- (C) rode her bike
- (D) studied

7. Carl called the _____ because he has _____.
- (A) doctor's office . . a fever
- (B) doctor's office . . a toothache
- (C) dentist's office . . a fever
- (D) dentist's office . . a toothache

Choose the correct answer to complete the conversation.

Example:

_____ Doctor Carter, please?

Ⓐ Are you
Ⓑ This is
Ⓒ May you speak with
● May I speak with

8. _____

Ⓐ Who's calling?
Ⓑ Who called?
Ⓒ Who do you call?
Ⓓ How do you feel?

9. _____ Ted Rogers. I have a terrible backache.

Ⓐ You are
Ⓑ He's
Ⓒ This is
Ⓓ Hello

10. I'm _____ to hear that.

Ⓐ glad
Ⓑ fine
Ⓒ okay
Ⓓ sorry

11. Can I _____?

Ⓐ seem to be the problem
Ⓑ make an appointment
Ⓒ feel fine
Ⓓ what's the matter

12. Yes. Please _____ tomorrow at 2:00.

Ⓐ hear that
Ⓑ feel okay
Ⓒ come in
Ⓓ get it

13. This is an emergency! My grandfather _____!

Ⓐ is very tired
Ⓑ has a cold
Ⓒ is very sick
Ⓓ has a toothache

14. _____

Ⓐ How does he feel today?
Ⓑ How did he get it?
Ⓒ Can you come in next Thursday?
Ⓓ What's the matter?

15. I don't know. He ate dinner, and now he feels _____. And he can't talk.

Ⓐ sorry
Ⓑ so-so
Ⓒ terrible
Ⓓ not so good

Okay. An ambulance is on the way.

8 Ⓐ Ⓑ Ⓒ Ⓓ 10 Ⓐ Ⓑ Ⓒ Ⓓ 12 Ⓐ Ⓑ Ⓒ Ⓓ 14 Ⓐ Ⓑ Ⓒ Ⓓ
9 Ⓐ Ⓑ Ⓒ Ⓓ 11 Ⓐ Ⓑ Ⓒ Ⓓ 13 Ⓐ Ⓑ Ⓒ Ⓓ 15 Ⓐ Ⓑ Ⓒ Ⓓ

Go to the next page ⟶

C READING: Over-the-Counter Medications

Read the drug store directory. Choose the correct answer to complete each conversation.

DISCOUNT MEDICAL PHARMACY
STORE DIRECTORY

	Aisle
ASPIRIN	1
COUGH SYRUP	2
EAR DROPS	3
COLD MEDICINE	4
THROAT LOZENGES	5
ANTACID TABLETS	6

Can you help me? I need something for a sore throat.

16. Look in _____.
   Ⓐ Aisle 1
   Ⓑ Aisle 2
   Ⓒ Aisle 5
   Ⓓ Aisle 6

Excuse me. Do you have aspirin and other medicine for a headache?

17. Yes. Look in _____.
   Ⓐ Aisle 1
   Ⓑ Aisle 3
   Ⓒ Aisle 4
   Ⓓ Aisle 6

Excuse me. I'm looking for medicine for a stomachache.

18. _____
   Ⓐ Ear drops are in Aisle 3.
   Ⓑ Antacid tablets are in Aisle 6.
   Ⓒ Throat lozenges are in Aisle 5.
   Ⓓ Cold medicine is in Aisle 4.

D LISTENING ASSESSMENT

Read and listen to the questions. Then listen to the conversation at the drug store, and answer the questions.

19. What's the matter with the person?
   Ⓐ She can't hear that.
   Ⓑ She sings on the weekend.
   Ⓒ She's in Aisle Two.
   Ⓓ She has a sore throat.

20. What's she going to buy?
   Ⓐ Cough syrup.
   Ⓑ Throat lozenges.
   Ⓒ Cough syrup and throat lozenges.
   Ⓓ Cold medicine.

....

16 Ⓐ Ⓑ Ⓒ Ⓓ   18 Ⓐ Ⓑ Ⓒ Ⓓ   20 Ⓐ Ⓑ Ⓒ Ⓓ

17 Ⓐ Ⓑ Ⓒ Ⓓ   19 Ⓐ Ⓑ Ⓒ Ⓓ

Go to the next page ⟩

E DRUG LABELS, DOSAGES, & FILLING/REFILLING PRESCRIPTIONS

For each conversation in the drug store, choose the correct medicine.

tsp. = teaspoon   1x / day = once a day
tab. = tablet   2x / day = twice a day
cap. = capsule   3x / day = 3 times a day

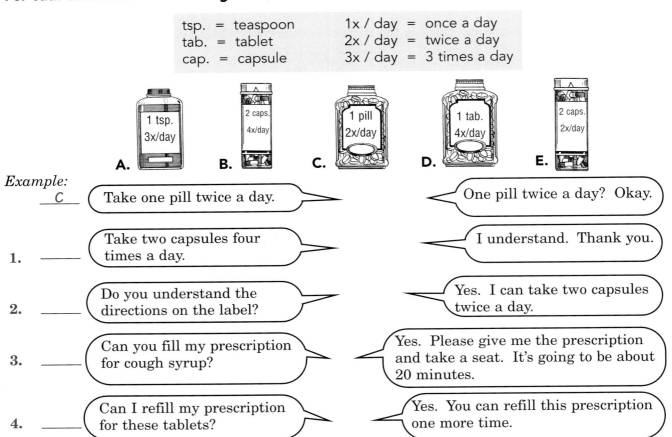

A.   B.   C.   D.   E.

Example:

___C___   Take one pill twice a day.   One pill twice a day? Okay.

1. ___   Take two capsules four times a day.   I understand. Thank you.

2. ___   Do you understand the directions on the label?   Yes. I can take two capsules twice a day.

3. ___   Can you fill my prescription for cough syrup?   Yes. Please give me the prescription and take a seat. It's going to be about 20 minutes.

4. ___   Can I refill my prescription for these tablets?   Yes. You can refill this prescription one more time.

F INTERPRETING A FAHRENHEIT THERMOMETER & A DOSAGE CUP

Fill in the thermometer to show a normal body temperature of 98.6° F. (98.6 degrees Fahrenheit).

For each drug label, fill in the correct amount of medicine in the dosage cup.

G WRITING ASSESSMENT

Write about your dinner yesterday (or another day). What did you eat? Where? Who cooked the dinner? Who ate with you? Who washed the dishes? Write about it on a separate sheet of paper.

H SPEAKING ASSESSMENT

I can ask and answer these questions:

Ask Answer
☐ ☐ How do you feel today?
☐ ☐ What did you do yesterday?
☐ ☐ What did you eat yesterday?
☐ ☐ What did you drink yesterday?

STOP

A COMMON ACTIVITIES IN THE PAST

Choose the correct answer.

Example:

My friends and I _____ a movie last Saturday.
- (A) see
- (B) did see
- (C) saw
- (D) did saw   Ⓐ Ⓑ ● Ⓓ

1. He _____ a book yesterday.
   - (A) rode
   - (B) red
   - (C) did read
   - (D) read

2. I _____ a bath yesterday evening. I usually _____ a shower.
   - (A) took . . took
   - (B) took . . take
   - (C) take . . took
   - (D) take . . take

3. I usually _____ dinner for my family, but yesterday my children _____ dinner.
   - (A) make . . make
   - (B) made . . make
   - (C) make . . made
   - (D) made . . made

4. _____ lunch yesterday?
   - (A) Did she eat
   - (B) Did she ate
   - (C) She eat
   - (D) She ate

5. _____ to work today?
   - (A) Ms. Clark did drive
   - (B) Ms. Clark drove
   - (C) Did Ms. Clark drive
   - (D) Did Ms. Clark drove

6. _____ his homework last night?
   - (A) Did your brother
   - (B) Did your brother did
   - (C) Did your brother do
   - (D) Do your brother did

7. What time _____ this morning?
   - (A) you got up
   - (B) you did get up
   - (C) got up you
   - (D) did you get up

8. _____ to school yesterday?
   - (A) How do they go
   - (B) How they do go
   - (C) How did they go
   - (D) How they did go

9. _____ at the supermarket?
   - (A) What did they buy
   - (B) What they buy
   - (C) What did they bought
   - (D) What they bought

10. Did you have a big breakfast today?
    - (A) Yes, I do.
    - (B) No, I don't.
    - (C) Yes, they did.
    - (D) No, I didn't.

11. Do you and your sister go to school every day?
    - (A) Yes, she does.
    - (B) Yes, we do.
    - (C) Yes, she did.
    - (D) Yes, we did.

....

1 Ⓐ Ⓑ Ⓒ Ⓓ   4 Ⓐ Ⓑ Ⓒ Ⓓ   7 Ⓐ Ⓑ Ⓒ Ⓓ   10 Ⓐ Ⓑ Ⓒ Ⓓ

2 Ⓐ Ⓑ Ⓒ Ⓓ   5 Ⓐ Ⓑ Ⓒ Ⓓ   8 Ⓐ Ⓑ Ⓒ Ⓓ   11 Ⓐ Ⓑ Ⓒ Ⓓ

3 Ⓐ Ⓑ Ⓒ Ⓓ   6 Ⓐ Ⓑ Ⓒ Ⓓ   9 Ⓐ Ⓑ Ⓒ Ⓓ

B GRAMMAR IN CONTEXT: Apologizing for Lateness at Work

Choose the correct answer to complete the conversation.

Example:

_____ I'm late.
- (A) You're sorry
- ● I'm sorry
- (C) He's sorry
- (D) She's sorry

12. _____
- (A) What's going to happen?
- (B) What's happening?
- (C) What happened?
- (D) What happens?

13. I _____ late and I _____ the bus.
- (A) get up . . miss
- (B) did get up . . did miss
- (C) got up . . miss
- (D) got up . . missed

14. _____
- (A) You understand.
- (B) I see.
- (C) You're sorry.
- (D) I have good excuses.

C READING: Safety Procedures

Read the safety posters. Then answer the questions on the next page.

Duck, Cover, & Hold!

What to Do At School During an Earthquake

IN A CLASSROOM:

Duck! Get down under a desk or table. (Don't go near windows, bookcases, or other tall furniture.)

Cover! Cover your head with the desk or table. Cover your eyes. (Put your face into your arm.)

Hold! Hold on to the desk or table so it stays over your head. (Furniture can move during an earthquake.)

IN THE HALL:

Drop! Sit on the floor near an inside wall. Get down on your knees. Lean over to rest on your elbows. Put your hands together behind your neck. Put your face down.

OUTSIDE:

Don't go near buildings or walls. Sit down, or use the "Drop" position.

Stop, Drop, Cover, & Roll!

What to Do If Your Clothing Is on Fire

Stop! Stop where you are. Don't run.

Drop! Drop to the ground.

Cover! Cover your face.

Roll! Roll from side to side, over and over, until the fire goes out.

15. Mr. Gardner's English class had an earthquake drill in their classroom today. What did the students do first?
- Ⓐ They covered their eyes.
- Ⓑ They went near the windows.
- Ⓒ They got down under their desks.
- Ⓓ They moved the furniture.

16. What didn't the students do during the earthquake drill?
- Ⓐ They didn't cover their heads.
- Ⓑ They didn't hold on to their desks.
- Ⓒ They didn't cover their eyes.
- Ⓓ They didn't roll from side to side.

17. What did students in the hall do during the earthquake drill?
- Ⓐ They went to their classrooms.
- Ⓑ They went outside.
- Ⓒ They sat down near an inside wall.
- Ⓓ They rested on the floor.

18. Your clothing is on fire. What are you going to do?
- Ⓐ Duck, cover, and hold.
- Ⓑ Stop, drop, cover, and roll.
- Ⓒ Cover my head with a desk or table.
- Ⓓ Run to a window.

Ⓓ LISTENING ASSESSMENT

Read and listen to the questions. Then listen to the story, and answer the questions.

19. Which meals did she have yesterday?
- Ⓐ She had breakfast and dinner.
- Ⓑ She had lunch and dinner.
- Ⓒ She had breakfast and lunch.
- Ⓓ She had breakfast, lunch, and dinner.

20. What did she do at the mall?
- Ⓐ She met her friend Bob.
- Ⓑ She met her mother.
- Ⓒ She ate lunch.
- Ⓓ She bought a gift.

Ⓔ WRITING & GRAMMAR ASSESSMENT

Example:

Did your parents wash their windows today?

_____ No, they didn't. _____

_____ They washed their car. _____

1. Did Sally go to the doctor this afternoon?

_____

_____

2. Did Mr. Lee drive a taxi today?

_____

_____

3. Did the students take the train to the zoo?

_____

_____

F EYE CONTACT & GESTURES

For each sentence, choose the correct picture.

A

B

C

D

E

F

1. "I understand." _____

2. "I don't understand." _____

3. "I'm happy to meet you." _____

4. "I have a question." _____

5. "I'd like to introduce my friend." _____

6. "I don't know." _____

G WRITING ASSESSMENT

What did you do yesterday? Write a paragraph about all the things you did. Use a separate sheet of paper.

H SPEAKING ASSESSMENT

I can ask and answer these questions about common activities (using full sentences):

Ask Answer

☐ ☐ What did you do yesterday?
☐ ☐ Did you study English yesterday?
☐ ☐ What time did you go to bed last night?
☐ ☐ What time did you get up today?
☐ ☐ Did you have breakfast this morning?
☐ ☐ What did you have for breakfast?
☐ ☐ How did you get to school today?
☐ ☐ What did you do last weekend?

STOP

Name _____

Date _____ Class _____

A BASIC FOODS & COMMON CONTAINERS

1. Do you like _____?
   Yes, I do.
   - Ⓐ cookies
   - Ⓑ pie
   - Ⓒ spaghetti
   - Ⓓ cake

2. Do you like _____?
   No, I don't.
   - Ⓐ cheese
   - Ⓑ spaghetti
   - Ⓒ cereal
   - Ⓓ ice cream

3. Where are the _____?
   They're over there.
   - Ⓐ cake
   - Ⓑ bread
   - Ⓒ cookies
   - Ⓓ cheese

4. What kind of _____ do
   you like?
   I like apple _____.
   - Ⓐ pie . . pie
   - Ⓑ cake . . cake
   - Ⓒ bread . . bread
   - Ⓓ cookies . . cookies

5. What did you have for
   dessert?
   We had a pint of _____.
   - Ⓐ cookies
   - Ⓑ ice cream
   - Ⓒ soda
   - Ⓓ milk

6. What did you buy at the
   supermarket?
   We bought a loaf of _____.
   - Ⓐ cheese
   - Ⓑ cereal
   - Ⓒ bread
   - Ⓓ cake

7. What did they drink with
   their lunch?
   They drank a bottle of _____.
   - Ⓐ milk
   - Ⓑ pie
   - Ⓒ cheese
   - Ⓓ soda

8. What did you buy at the
   grocery store?
   I bought a gallon of _____.
   - Ⓐ soda
   - Ⓑ milk
   - Ⓒ pie
   - Ⓓ cereal

9. What did you get at the
   supermarket?
   I got a pound of _____.
   - Ⓐ cheese
   - Ⓑ bread
   - Ⓒ ice cream
   - Ⓓ cereal

10. What do you want from
    the supermarket?
    Please get a box of _____
    for breakfast.
    - Ⓐ milk
    - Ⓑ cereal
    - Ⓒ pie
    - Ⓓ cheese

1 Ⓐ Ⓑ Ⓒ Ⓓ   3 Ⓐ Ⓑ Ⓒ Ⓓ   5 Ⓐ Ⓑ Ⓒ Ⓓ   7 Ⓐ Ⓑ Ⓒ Ⓓ   9 Ⓐ Ⓑ Ⓒ Ⓓ
2 Ⓐ Ⓑ Ⓒ Ⓓ   4 Ⓐ Ⓑ Ⓒ Ⓓ   6 Ⓐ Ⓑ Ⓒ Ⓓ   8 Ⓐ Ⓑ Ⓒ Ⓓ   10 Ⓐ Ⓑ Ⓒ Ⓓ

Go to the next page ⟶ **T55** ●

GRAMMAR IN CONTEXT: System of Weights Using Ounces & Pounds

Choose the correct answer to complete the conversation.

16 ounces = 1 pound (lb.)

11. How much is this _____?
- Ⓐ bread
- Ⓑ cake
- Ⓒ cheese
- Ⓓ pie

12. It's _____ per pound.
- Ⓐ ten cents
- Ⓑ ten dollars
- Ⓒ one dollar
- Ⓓ one hundred dollars

13. _____ half a pound, please?
- Ⓐ I have
- Ⓑ Have I
- Ⓒ I can have
- Ⓓ Can I have

14. _____ ounces? Okay.
- Ⓐ 4
- Ⓑ 8
- Ⓒ 12
- Ⓓ 16

15. _____ are the cookies? I want to buy two pounds.
- Ⓐ How much
- Ⓑ How many
- Ⓒ Who
- Ⓓ What

16. They're $6.00 per pound. That's going to be _____.
- Ⓐ $3.00
- Ⓑ $6.00
- Ⓒ $9.00
- Ⓓ $12.00

C **READING**

Read the story. Then answer the questions.

Alex Fernandez was born in El Salvador. He grew up in San Salvador, the capital city of his country. When Alex was fourteen years old, his family moved to the United States. First they lived in Dallas, Texas, and then they moved to Miami, Florida. Alex began high school in Texas. He was sad when his family moved. He liked his high school in Dallas, and he had many friends there. But Alex was also very happy in his new high school. He met many new friends there. Alex finished high school last year. Now he works in a restaurant at the Miami airport, and he studies at a computer school at night. Next year, he's going to go to college in Tampa, Florida. Alex is looking forward to next year and a very exciting future.

17. Where did Alex finish high school?
- Ⓐ In San Salvador.
- Ⓑ In Dallas.
- Ⓒ In Miami.
- Ⓓ In Tampa.

18. Which sentence is not correct?
- Ⓐ Alex finished high school.
- Ⓑ Alex has a job.
- Ⓒ Alex goes to a computer school.
- Ⓓ Alex goes to college.

11 Ⓐ Ⓑ Ⓒ Ⓓ   13 Ⓐ Ⓑ Ⓒ Ⓓ   15 Ⓐ Ⓑ Ⓒ Ⓓ   17 Ⓐ Ⓑ Ⓒ Ⓓ

12 Ⓐ Ⓑ Ⓒ Ⓓ   14 Ⓐ Ⓑ Ⓒ Ⓓ   16 Ⓐ Ⓑ Ⓒ Ⓓ   18 Ⓐ Ⓑ Ⓒ Ⓓ

Go to the next page ⟩

D LISTENING ASSESSMENT

Read and listen to the questions. Then listen to the commercial, and answer the questions.

19. What kind of product is this commercial about?
    - (A) Shampoo.
    - (B) Window cleaner.
    - (C) Floor wax.
    - (D) Vitamins

20. How did the person get the product?
    - (A) Some friends gave the person the product.
    - (B) The person got the product at a party.
    - (C) The person got the product at a store.
    - (D) The person got the product at work.

E FOOD ADS

Look at the advertisements for food. Answer the questions.

California Navel **Oranges** 3/$1

Skim Milk ONE GALLON $2⁴⁹ BUY 1 GET 1 FREE!

Imported Swiss Cheese $6⁵⁰ lb.

Compare + Save! **Fresh Lettuce** 2 for $3

1. How much are two heads of lettuce? _____

2. What's the price of three oranges? _____

3. What's the price of six oranges? _____

4. How much is a pound of Swiss cheese? _____

5. How much is half a pound of Swiss cheese? _____

6. How much are two gallons of milk? _____

F CLOZE READING

Read the story and circle the correct words.

I Went to Bed Early

I   go   (went)   did go   to bed early last night because I   was   were   am [1]   very

tired. My sister   wasn't   didn't   not [2]   go to bed early because she   has   have   had [3]

a lot of homework. She   did   do   does [4]   her homework for two hours, and then she

go   goes   went [5]   to bed.

G LEARNING SKILL: Categorizing

Write each word in the correct column.

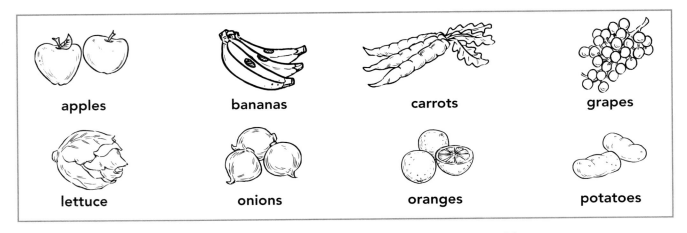

apples   bananas   carrots   grapes

lettuce   onions   oranges   potatoes

Fruits	Vegetables
apples	carrots

H WRITING ASSESSMENT

Write about your childhood. Where were you born? Where did you grow up? What did you look like? Where did you go to school? What did you do with your friends? (Use a separate sheet of paper.)

I SPEAKING ASSESSMENT

I can ask and answer these questions:

Ask Answer

☐ ☐ What day was it yesterday?
☐ ☐ What was yesterday's date?
☐ ☐ Where were you yesterday?
☐ ☐ Where were you born?
☐ ☐ Where did you grow up?

STOP

Listening Assessment Scripts

CHAPTER 1 TEST

Page T3, Section E

Read and listen to the questions.

18. What's her last name?
19. What's her phone number?
20. What's her address?

Now listen to the interview, and answer the questions.

A. What's your first name?
B. Susan.
A. What's your last name?
B. Keller.
A. How do you spell that?
B. K - E - L - L - E - R.
A. What's your address?
B. 86 Central Avenue.
A. What's your telephone number?
B. 861-2394.

CHAPTER 2 TEST

Page T8, Section D

Read and listen to the questions.

18. What's the principal's name?
19. Where's the teacher?
20. Which student is absent today?

Now listen to the conversation, and answer the questions.

A. Hello, students. My name is Mrs. Lane. I'm the principal.
B. Hello, Mrs. Lane.
A. Your English teacher, Mr. Wilson, is absent today.
B. Where's Mr. Wilson?
A. He's in the hospital.
B. What a shame!
A. Are all the students here today?
B. Everybody except Rosa.
A. Where's Rosa?
B. She's at the dentist.

CHAPTER 3 TEST

Page T10, Section C

Read and listen to the questions.

18. What are Mr. and Mrs. Baker doing?
19. What's Tommy doing?
20. Where are they today?

Now listen to the story, and answer the questions.

The Baker family is at the beach today. It's a beautiful day! Mr. Baker is reading the newspaper. Mrs. Baker is reading a book. Tommy Baker is swimming. Sally Baker is listening to music. The Baker family is very happy today. It's a beautiful day, and they're at the beach.

CHAPTER 4 TEST

Page T12, Section C

Read and listen to the questions.

18. What's Lisa doing?
19. What's Richard doing?
20. What are the children doing?

Now listen to the telephone conversation, and answer the questions.

A. Hello, Lisa? This is Susan. Are you busy?
B. Yes, I am.
A. What are you doing?
B. I'm washing my windows.
A. Oh. Is Richard busy?
B. Yes, he is. He's cooking.
A. What's he cooking?
B. He's cooking dinner.
A. Are your children busy?
B. Yes, they are. They're doing their homework.
A. It's a very busy day today!
B. Yes. It is.
A. Well, nice to talk with you.
B. Nice to talk with you, too.
A. Goodbye.

CHAPTER 5 TEST

Page T14, Section D

Read and listen to the questions.

18. How's the weather in Miami?
19. What's the temperature in Los Angeles?
20. How's the weather in New York?

Now listen to the weather report, and answer the questions.

Here is today's weather report. It's a beautiful day in Miami. It's sunny and hot. The temperature is 95 degrees Fahrenheit. And it's a beautiful day in Los Angeles. It's sunny and warm. The temperature is 80 degrees Fahrenheit. It isn't a beautiful day today in New York. It's raining. The temperature is 35 degrees Fahrenheit.

CHAPTER 6 TEST

Page T17, Section D

Read and listen to the questions.

18. What day is it?
19. What are his parents doing?
20. What's his grandfather doing?

Now listen to the story, and answer the questions.

Today is a very special day. It's my birthday, and all my family and friends are at my birthday party. My sister and brother are dancing with my friends in the living room. My mother and father are sitting with my grandmother in the kitchen. They're eating birthday cake. My grandfather is taking photographs. Everybody is having a good time. It's a very special day.

CHAPTER 7 TEST

Page T21, Section D

Read and listen to the questions.

18. How many bedrooms are there in the apartment?
19. How many bathrooms are there?
20. Where's the laundromat?

Now listen to the conversation, and answer the questions.

A. Is the apartment large?
B. Yes, it is. There are six rooms in the apartment.
A. How many bedrooms are there?
B. There are three bedrooms.
A. And how many bathrooms are there?
B. There's one bathroom.
A. Is there an elevator in the building?
B. Yes. There are two elevators.
A. Is the building in a convenient place?
B. Yes, it is. There's a supermarket next to the building, and there's a post office around the corner.
A. Is there a laundromat in the neighborhood?
B. Yes, there is. There's a laundromat across from the post office.

CHAPTER 8 TEST

Page T24, Section C

Read and listen to the questions.

18. Where is the conversation taking place?
19. What's the person looking for?
20. What size is the raincoat?

Now listen to the conversation, and answer the questions.

A. May I help you?
B. Yes, please. I'm looking for a green raincoat for my husband.
A. I'm sorry. All our raincoats are yellow.
B. That's okay.
A. What size are you looking for?
B. Hmm. I don't know.
A. Is your husband tall or short?
B. He's very tall.
A. Here's a nice raincoat.
B. What size is it?
A. It's large.
B. It's a very nice raincoat. Thanks very much.

CHAPTER 9 TEST

Page T30, Section C

Read and listen to the questions.

18. Where does she live?
19. What does she do at work?
20. What does she do at home?

Now listen to the conversation, and answer the questions.

A. What's your name?
B. My name is Sonia.
A. Where are you from?
B. I'm from Greece.
A. Where do you live?
B. I live in Dallas.
A. Where do you work?
B. I work in a restaurant.
A. What do you do at work?
B. I cook.
A. What do you do at home?
B. I read books, I watch TV, and I play the piano.

CHAPTER 10 TEST

Page T33, Section C

Read and listen to the questions.

17. What do they do on Tuesday?
18. Do they ride their bikes on Wednesday?
19. What do they do on Friday?
20. What do they do on the weekend?

Now listen to the story, and answer the questions.

My parents are very athletic people. They do a different kind of exercise or sport every day. On Monday they jog together. On Tuesday they play tennis together. On Wednesday my mother does yoga, and my father swims. On Thursday they ride their bikes together. On Friday my mother plays golf, and my father plays basketball. On Saturday and Sunday, they go to a health club together. They're very active people!

CHAPTER 11 TEST

Page T36, Section C

Read and listen to the questions.

18. How does this person look like her sister?
19. Where does the teacher live?
20. What do they do every day?

Now listen to the story, and answer the questions.

I look like my sister. We're both tall and thin. We both have blue eyes. We both have short brown hair. My hair is curly, and her hair is curly. My sister and I are very different. I'm a scientist. She's a teacher. I live in a small apartment in the city. She lives in a large apartment in the suburbs. On the weekend I rarely go out. I usually watch videos. My sister always goes out on the weekend. She often goes to parties with her friends. My sister and I talk on the telephone every day. Sometimes I call her, and sometimes she calls me. We're very close friends.

CHAPTER 12 TEST

Page T38, Section D

Read and listen to the questions.

17. What does Wanda do at the office?
18. Who cleans the office?
19. What's Nancy's job?
20. Where's Mrs. Kent?

Now listen to the conversation, and answer the questions.

A. Welcome to our office.
B. Thank you.
A. Let me introduce you to the employees here.
B. Okay.
A. This is George. He's the receptionist. He answers the telephone. And this is Wanda. She's the office assistant. She sorts the mail. This is Ken. He's our custodian. He cleans the office. Our secretary isn't here today. Her name is Nancy. She types all the letters, but she's sick today. She's at home with the flu. And our boss isn't here right now. Her name is Mrs. Kent. She's the president of our company. She's at the dentist this morning.

CHAPTER 13 TEST

Page T40, Section E

Read and listen to the questions.

18. Where is the job interview taking place?
19. What can David do?
20. David doesn't have one skill. What can't he do?

Now listen to the job interview, and answer the questions.

A. What's your name?
B. My name is David Simpson.
A. Nice to meet you, David.
B. Nice to meet you, too.
A. Tell me, David, what kind of job are you looking for here at our store?
B. I'm looking for a job as a salesperson.
A. Okay. Can you use a cash register?
B. Yes, I can.
A. Can you take inventory?
B. Yes, I can.
A. Can you talk to customers?
B. Yes, I can.
A. Can you operate business software on a computer?
B. No, I can't. But I can type.
A. Very good. Please fill out this application form.
B. Thank you.

CHAPTER 14 TEST

Page T44, Section D

Read and listen to the questions.

17. What's he going to do in March?
18. When is he going to begin to study at a computer school?
19. Where is he going to work?
20. How old is he going to be in June?

Now listen to the story, and answer the questions.

Next year is going to be a very interesting year. In January I'm going to start a new job at a big office in the center of the city. In March I'm going to move to a new apartment building. In June I'm going to celebrate my thirtieth birthday. I'm going to have a big birthday party. In September I'm going to begin to study at night in a computer school. In November I'm going to get married. In December my wife and I are going to visit Honolulu. It's going to be a very busy and interesting year!

CHAPTER 15 TEST

Page T49, Section D

Read and listen to the questions.

19. What's the matter with the person?
20. What's she going to buy?

Now listen to the conversation at the drug store, and answer the questions.

A. Can you help me?
B. Yes?
A. I feel terrible.
B. What's the matter?
A. I have a terrible sore throat.
B. I'm sorry to hear that. How did you get it?
A. I sang all weekend.
B. Oh. Are you a singer?
A. Yes. What do you have for a sore throat?
B. Thaxton Throat Lozenges are very good for a sore throat. They're in Aisle Two between the cough syrup and the cold medicine.
A. Thanks very much.

CHAPTER 16 TEST

Page T53, Section D

Read and listen to the questions.

19. Which meals did she have yesterday?
20. What did she do at the mall?

Now listen to the story, and answer the questions.

I had a very busy day yesterday. I got up early and went jogging in the park. Then I took a quick shower. I didn't have breakfast. I took the bus to the library. I studied there, and I also read the newspaper. I met my friend Bob at the library. We walked to a restaurant and had lunch. After lunch I took the bus to the mall and I went shopping. I bought a gift for my mother. Her birthday is next Tuesday. Then I went home, had a quick dinner, watched TV, and went to bed. I had a very busy day!

CHAPTER 17 TEST

Page T57, Section D

Read and listen to the questions.

19. What kind of product is this commercial about?
20. How did the person get the product?

Now listen to the commercial, and answer the questions.

I had a problem with my hair. It was dirty and dull. I was embarrassed. I didn't go out. I didn't go to parties. Then my friends at work recommended Sunshine Plus. I went to the store and bought some. Now I use Sunshine Plus every day, and my hair isn't dirty and dull. It's clean and shiny. I'm not embarrassed any more. I go out, and I go to parties. Try Sunshine Plus today!